MARGARITAVILLE
THE COOKBOOK

MARGARITAVILLE
THE COOKBOOK

RELAXED RECIPES FOR A TASTE OF PARADISE

CARLO SERNAGLIA
and JULIA TURSHEN

FOREWORD BY JIMMY BUFFETT

Food photography by Beatriz da Costa

Lifestyle photography by Ryan Joseph of Ryan Joseph Photographs

ST. MARTIN'S PRESS
NEW YORK

www.stmartins.com
www.margaritaville.com

Design by Rita Sowins / Sowins Design

Food stylist: Frances Luard

Contents

SALADS AND SOUPS

SIDE DISHES

Foreword

The next best thing to eating a great meal is reading about one . . . and thumbing through pictures of well-prepared food! I probably have as many cookbooks as I have travel guides stuck away on my bookshelves. At times, Catholic guilt comes upon me (clean up before the maid gets here), and I will launch into a semi-scorched-earth reconnoitering of my office, just coiled to grab useless and discarded things that have collected from my travels. In that process, though, my cookbooks get a "hall pass."

Carlo Sernaglia's book will have a prime spot in my collection because I know the story behind his success. Like any journey you undertake to truly master something, the adventure can be long and failure a part of the process. I have shared many stories over many meals with Carlo. Italy to South Florida via Venezuela is almost a Columbus comparison, but there is a slight difference. The Admiral of the Oceans wasn't quite sure where he landed. Carlo was. He arrived in Caracas, a lawyer by trade, but a nomad at heart. It didn't take him long to realize that being a legal beagle was not his calling. So off he sailed to the island of Los Roques, where he of course ran into a runaway Sicilian architect. And over a couple of

Pampero rums, the Italians figured it all out (or so they thought!): Let's open the only classy restaurant on the island and make a fortune! It didn't work. But that did not stop Carlo. William Faulkner said, "You cannot swim for new horizons until you have courage to lose sight of the shore." So after three years of adventure (and political turmoil) our sailor landed on yet another foreign shore. Good-bye Venezuela . . . Hello South Florida!

It did not take Carlo long to reinvent himself on a new beach, from hotel chef to private chef to Margaritaville. Running that kind of gauntlet requires trust in the universe, and Carlo's passion, persistence, and pure joy rewarded him, and us. His passion for making great meals for appreciative diners is authentic, infectious, and inspiring. Nothing illustrates this more than his amazing perception of how to creatively deal with the lionfish problem in our coastal waters. Be sure and read that part of the story!

So enjoy digesting this book; there's a lot more in it than just recipes. You will learn how to make Lionfish Carpaccio, Cuban Meat Loaf Survival Sandwiches, and Paella del Mar, but more important, you will have an invaluable recipe as to how to live life.

JIMMY BUFFETT

Introduction

More than forty years after it began, MARGARITAVILLE, a synonym for paradise, is still all about kicking back and having a great time. And food is at the center of that feeling. It's about time we put all of our favorite recipes in one place, don't you think? Welcome to our cookbook.

Let's go back to the beginning. Margaritaville has been a state of mind since 1977. What started as a song, the one we all know and can't stop humming for days after we hear it, has steadily evolved into a company and a community that evoke a distinctly magical, supremely relaxed feeling. Now, for the first time ever, we are excited to invite you into Margaritaville through our cookbook. We've filled these pages with our favorite recipes and the stories behind them.

This book is all about the laid-back attitude, undeniably good food and drinks, and all-around lifestyle Margaritaville offers. It's organized into eight chapters (Breakfast; Appetizers; Salads and Soups; Burgers, Sandwiches & Hot Dogs; Main Dishes; Side Dishes; Desserts; and Drinks) that take you through the course of the day and beyond. The recipes have a ton of variety since they reflect the fun places we all love to eat. From food that's prepared on the beach to meals to enjoy while tailgating, you'll get everything from our greatest hits (like Volcano Nachos, page 36, and Cheeseburgers in Paradise, page 126) to the elevated food we serve at the award-winning JWB Prime Steak and Seafood at our Hollywood Beach Resort. Just wait until you try recipes from our wonderful concept chef, Carlo Sernaglia, like the fresh Paradise Ceviche on page 75. We've said that our food can be tied to our "Gulf Coast

Floribbean" roots, and you'll see so many recipes influenced by Key West, where we started, and New Orleans and the Caribbean, where we landed next.

All the recipes emphasize simple techniques and high-quality ingredients. We brought on bestselling cookbook author Julia Turshen to make sure the recipes are easy to follow. The recipes include wonderful, thoughtful details like serving ever-so-spicy Peppadew peppers with crispy fried calamari to easily provide a bit of spark (head over to page 57 for the recipe).

The recipes reflect our regional and international range. Wherever we open a new location, our goal is to operate as respectful guests looking to celebrate local culture and not impose upon it. Our menus and memories have come to include a wonderful variety of items that make the book rich with influences and stories (Jerk Chicken from Jamaica on page 190, key lime pie straight from the source in Key West on page 272, and Jimmy's Jammin' Jambalaya, which is a love letter to New Orleans, on page 225). The recipes and stories make it easy to escape without ever leaving your home.

The book is especially useful if you enjoy entertaining (think: a clambake that you can either do on the beach or just in a large pot in your kitchen over on page 199). There is a real social aspect to everything we do, and we like to create the kind of atmosphere that feels like the hug you give to a stranger at a baseball game when a home run is hit out of the park. Everyone is just happy to be there, together, in the moment. Whether you're having just one friend over to watch a movie, a small gathering, or a big blow-out party, we're all about that feeling. Check out all the party suggestions (page 320) for some really fun ideas, including complete menus.

When we set out to create this book, our goal was to provide not only everything you expect from us, but even more. We hope you enjoy reading it and cooking from it as much as we enjoyed making it. Fins up!

"It's in the tropics somewhere between the Port of Indecision and Southwest of Disorder, but no parallels of latitude or longitude mark the spot exactly. You don't have to be a navigator to get there. Palm trees provide the camouflage. Ocean breezes bring the seaplanes and sailboats, tourists and travelers. Passports are not required. Island music rules. No waiting on lines for anything. There is a beach and a thatched roof bar perched on the edge of a turquoise sea where you can always find a barstool. There are lots of lies and loads of stories. It's a comical concoction that blends together like tequila, salt, and limes. Where is Margaritaville? It's in your mind. . . ."

—JIMMY BUFFETT

Breakfast

"DRINKIN' LOTS OF CARROT JUICE AND SOAKIN' UP RAYS . . ."

In Margaritaville, breakfast is the first opportunity of the day to feel relaxed and taken care of. For us, mornings aren't about being rushed out the door or running late to work. They're about drinking coffee with your feet in the sand or reading the newspaper in a hammock. While we know not every single morning will be the most leisurely, we're always looking for ways to start every day in the Margaritaville state of mind. That might mean fixing a quick smoothie with island flavors like coconut and pineapple to take with you on your commute so you can close your eyes and pretend your feet are on the sand. Or maybe it's about inviting your family over on a weekend morning for a tall stack of Triple B (Buttermilk, Blueberry, and Banana) Pancakes (page 27) or a big platter of Huevos Rancheros (page 16). This chapter includes all these plus so much more. From our famous Key West Omelet (page 19) to new favorites like Key Lime Yogurt with Graham Cracker Granola (page 12), this chapter will have you going to bed dreaming of getting into the kitchen in the morning.

Pineapple and Coconut Milk Smoothie

Basically a piña colada for breakfast, this smoothie could not be faster or easier to make, thanks in particular to the frozen pineapple. It requires no peeling or chopping and it also acts as both fruit and ice so it makes the smoothie chilled and thick without any risk of diluting it. Speaking of piña coladas, a splash of rum and a squeeze of lime would not be terrible here. . . . Drink these while looking at a view.

One 13.5-ounce can low-fat coconut milk, well shaken

One 10-ounce package frozen pineapple

1 cup pineapple juice

4 small wedges fresh pineapple, for serving (optional)

Place the coconut milk, frozen pineapple, and pineapple juice in a blender and puree until smooth. Divide among four glasses, garnish with fresh pineapple if you'd like, and serve immediately.

Key Lime Yogurt with Graham Cracker Granola

Serves 4

With all the familiar flavors of key lime pie translated into breakfast, this crunchy granola, made with oats and crushed-up graham crackers, gets sweetened with a little bit of coconut and honey. It's just the thing to balance creamy, tart yogurt that's swirled with a bit of key lime juice. A shower of berries makes this decidedly healthy and also really beautiful. This makes more than enough granola for four servings. Leftovers can be stored in an airtight container at room temperature for at least a week and make for a good snack or ice cream topping.

One 4½-ounce sleeve of graham crackers, crushed

1 cup old-fashioned rolled oats

½ cup unsweetened shredded coconut

3 tablespoons unsalted butter, melted

2 tablespoons honey

Large pinch of kosher salt

2 cups plain yogurt

¼ cup key lime juice (preferably Nellie & Joe's)

2 cups mixed berries

Preheat the oven to 350°F. Line a rimmed baking sheet with parchment paper.

Place the crushed graham crackers, oats, coconut, butter, honey, and salt in a large bowl and stir everything together. Transfer the mixture to the prepared baking sheet. Bake, stirring now and then, until the oats and coconut are golden brown and the whole thing smells nutty and wonderful, about 15 minutes. Set the granola aside to cool (it will crisp as it cools).

Meanwhile, place the yogurt and key lime juice in a large bowl and whisk together.

Divide the key lime yogurt and the berries among four bowls or glasses. Sprinkle with as much granola as you like and serve immediately.

Baked Boatmeal Squares with Blueberries and Coconut

Makes 9 squares

Baked almost like a bar cookie and cut into squares for serving, this oatmeal is both portable and can also be made ahead and enjoyed at room temperature or warmed up. In other words, you can make a batch one day and have breakfast for the whole week. We love taking this with us for a day on the boat (boatmeal!), but it's also great for breakfast on the go, whether you're headed to school or work. The blueberries can be swapped out for chopped apples or raspberries and the coconut can be swapped out for any type of chopped nut or dried fruit. These are also wonderful for desserts, served warm with a scoop of vanilla ice cream.

Baking spray

2 cups old-fashioned rolled oats

1 teaspoon kosher salt

2 teaspoons ground cinnamon

1½ teaspoons baking powder

⅓ cup packed dark brown sugar

2 large eggs, beaten

1¼ cups whole milk

2 teaspoons pure vanilla extract

1 cup fresh or frozen (no need to defrost) blueberries

½ cup unsweetened shredded coconut

Preheat the oven to 350°F. Spray an 9 x 13-inch square baking pan with baking spray. Line the bottom with parchment paper cut to fit and spray that, too, just to be safe.

Place the oats, salt, cinnamon, and baking powder in a large bowl and stir to combine. Add the brown sugar, eggs, milk, and vanilla and stir well. Stir in the blueberries and coconut.

Transfer the mixture to the prepared baking pan and spread it into an even layer.

Bake until the oatmeal is firm to the touch and light golden brown on top, about 25 minutes. Let the oatmeal cool in the pan for at least 15 minutes, then transfer it to a cutting board. Cut it into 9 even squares. Serve warm or at room temperature. Leftovers can be stored in an airtight container in the refrigerator for up to 3 days or wrapped well and frozen for up to 3 months (defrost and warm in a toaster oven before eating).

Huevos Rancheros

Serves 4

The chorizo in these huevos rancheros makes them incredibly savory and satisfying, but if you prefer a vegetarian version, simply leave it out. You could add some sautéed onions and peppers, if you'd like, or just keep it simple with beans and scrambled eggs. Either way, don't skip the broiling. The melted cheese is the best part! The cured chorizo will enhance the smokiness of the dish, but fresh chorizo works equally well. Serve on the weekend after a big night.

2 tablespoons neutral oil (such as canola or vegetable), for frying

½ pound cured chorizo sausage, finely diced

8 large eggs

Kosher salt

Freshly ground black pepper

1 cup grated white cheddar cheese

8 corn tortillas, warmed

1½ cups drained Fajita Black Beans (page 255), warmed

1 cup Pico de Gallo (page 238)

½ cup crumbled queso blanco cheese

1 avocado, pitted, peeled, and thinly sliced

½ cup sour cream

Small handful of fresh cilantro, coarsely chopped

1 lime, cut into wedges, for serving

Place the oil in a large nonstick skillet set over medium-high heat. Add the chorizo and cook, stirring now and then, until it's browned and crisp and has released all its fat, about 5 minutes. Use a slotted spoon to transfer the chorizo to a plate and set it aside. Leave the fat in the skillet and return it to medium heat. Crack the eggs into the skillet in a single layer (work in batches, if necessary) and sprinkle each with a large pinch of salt and a few grinds of black pepper. Sprinkle the eggs with the cheddar cheese and cover the pan. Cook until the cheese is melted and the egg whites are set, about 2 minutes.

(continued)

Place the tortillas on serving platter (or in a large skillet, which is a fun way to serve these). Top each tortilla with a fried, cheesy egg. Divide the reserved chorizo, beans, pico de gallo, queso blanco, avocado, sour cream, and cilantro among the eggs. Serve immediately with lime wedges for squeezing over the dish.

Key West Omelet

You could say Key West, Florida, is our Graceland, so it should be no surprise that key lime juice, the Keys' most distinctive flavor, appears in so many of our signature dishes. This omelet, full of shrimp and crab and topped with decadent Key Lime Hollandaise sauce, makes any morning feel like a weekend.

6 medium shrimp, peeled and deveined

1 tablespoon neutral oil (such as canola or vegetable)

2 tablespoons fresh or pasteurized jumbo lump crabmeat

Kosher salt

3 large eggs, beaten

¼ cup Key Lime Hollandaise (recipe follows), warmed

1 tablespoon minced fresh chives

Coarsely chop 3 of the shrimp (leave the other 3 whole). Place the oil in a small nonstick skillet set over medium heat. Add both the chopped and whole shrimp and the crab and season with a large pinch of salt. Cook, stirring, until the shrimp are just firm to the touch and opaque, about 3 minutes. Transfer the 3 whole shrimp to a plate and set aside. Add the eggs and another large pinch of salt to the skillet. When the eggs on the bottom begin to set, after about 30 seconds, use a rubber spatula to gently pull the sides of the cooked eggs toward the center of the pan. Repeat the process until the eggs are just cooked through, about 3 minutes. Carefully flip half the omelet over itself to form a half-moon and slide it onto a plate.

Top the omelet with the reserved shrimp, the hollandaise, and chives and serve immediately.

Key Lime Hollandaise

Using a blender to do all the difficult work of emulsifying, we make this hollandaise sauce the modern way. We like to clarify the butter for the sauce, which we walk you through in the recipe, since it leaves you with butter that tastes, if you can believe it, even more like butter. It's a chef-y trick from Carlo, and he explains that by getting rid of the milk solids (the white proteins that naturally separate from the butter when you cook it), you're left with clear butter that's truly like the essence of butter. If that didn't sound good enough, we add a good dose of key lime juice to flavor the sauce, because no matter where we are, we never stray far from Key West.

16 tablespoons (2 sticks) unsalted butter, cut into large cubes

3 large egg yolks

3 tablespoons key lime juice (preferably Nellie & Joe's)

Pinch of kosher salt

Pinch of cayenne pepper

1 tablespoon warm water

Line a small sieve with a coffee filter or a piece of cheesecloth and set it over a medium bowl.

Place the butter in a small pot set over high heat. Once it melts, let the butter cook until the white milk proteins float to the surface, about 3 minutes. Once the butter boils, reduce the heat to medium and cook until the white milk proteins sink to the bottom of the pot. Strain the butter through the coffee filter or cheesecloth and discard the solids. Set the warm, melted clarified butter aside.

Place the egg yolks, key lime juice, salt, and cayenne in a blender and puree until combined. With the machine running, slowly drizzle in the clarified butter (make sure it's still warm) to form a thick, emulsified sauce. Add the water and blend to combine. Serve the sauce warm from the blender (it can sit in the blender for up to 30 minutes before serving).

South Florida Eggs Benedict

Serves 4

The ultimate weekend brunch, eggs Benedict are always a hit, but the Key Lime Hollandaise sauce makes this version especially memorable. For a version of eggs Florentine, try swapping out the Canadian bacon for a spoonful of warm JWB Creamed Spinach (page 253).

1 tablespoon neutral oil (such as canola or vegetable), for frying

8 slices Canadian bacon

1 tablespoon distilled white vinegar

2 teaspoons kosher salt

8 large eggs

4 English muffins, split and toasted

1 cup Key Lime Hollandaise (page 20), warmed

Small handful of fresh chives, minced

Large pinch of dried red chile flakes, for serving (optional)

Place the oil in a large nonstick skillet set over medium heat. Add the Canadian bacon in an even layer and cook, turning the slices a few times, until warmed through and lightly browned in spots, about 4 minutes. Keep the Canadian bacon warm over low heat.

Meanwhile, place 8 cups water in a large saucepan set over high heat and bring to a boil. Lower the heat to keep the water at a simmer and stir in the vinegar and the salt. Working with one egg at a time, crack each egg into a small bowl. Stir the water gently to create a whirlpool and, while gently stirring, carefully slip the egg into the water. Repeat the process as quickly as possible with the remaining eggs and work in batches as necessary to makes sure the eggs stay separate (this will be determined by the size of your pan). Poach the eggs until they're barely firm to the touch, about 3 minutes. Remove the eggs with a slotted spoon and blot dry on paper towels.

Place the English muffins on plates, toasted-sides up. Place a slice of warm Canadian bacon and a poached egg on top of each half. Drizzle the hollandaise over everything, top with the chives and chile flakes, and serve immediately.

Spicy Breakfast Quesadillas

We love a breakfast quesadilla, but it's a hard thing to make for a crowd since you normally have to wait for one to finish before you can make another in your skillet. Enter two hot baking sheets. By heating them up in the oven and baking the quesadillas between them, you can easily make a bunch of quesadillas at the same time. Of course, if you're just making one for yourself, you can go ahead and make it in a skillet on the stovetop. Simply sear the quesadilla in a bit of oil or butter until browned on both sides and the cheese is melted (just like making a grilled cheese).

2 tablespoons unsalted butter

8 large eggs, beaten

½ teaspoon kosher salt

Cooking spray

Four 10-inch flour tortillas

½ cup coarsely grated Monterey Jack cheese

½ cup coarsely grated sharp cheddar cheese

3 tablespoons drained pickled jalapeños, coarsely chopped

3 tablespoons minced fresh cilantro

1 cup Pico de Gallo (page 238), for serving

Preheat the oven to 400°F. Place two baking sheets in the oven to heat up.

Place the butter in a large nonstick skillet set over medium heat. Once it melts, add the eggs and salt and cook, stirring with a rubber spatula, until the eggs are just set, about 4 minutes.

Take one of the hot baking sheets out of the oven and spray with cooking spray. Place the tortillas on the pan and evenly sprinkle both of the cheeses over the surface of each tortilla. Evenly divide the scrambled eggs among the tortillas, being sure to put them on only half of each tortilla. Top the eggs with the pickled jalapeños and cilantro. Fold each tortilla in half to form a half-moon. Spray the top of each quesadilla with cooking spray and stack the other hot baking sheets on top on them so that the quesadillas make contact on both sides with the hot baking sheets.

Place the quesadillas, sandwiched between the baking sheets, in the oven and bake until both sides are golden brown and the cheese is melted, about 10 minutes.

Cut each quesadilla into wedges and serve immediately, with the pico de gallo on top.

Triple B (Buttermilk, Blueberry, and Banana) Pancakes

Serves 4 to 6

While these classic buttermilk pancakes have both blueberries and bananas in them, you could easily just do one type of fruit. Or try other mix-ins such as strawberries, peaches, walnuts, granola, coconut, and/or even chocolate chips. If you don't have a griddle and can't make more than a couple of pancakes at the same time, keep the finished ones warm in a 250°F oven while you cook the rest of the batch. This is the best thing to make for your family on the weekend.

2 cups all-purpose flour

1 tablespoon baking powder

½ teaspoon kosher salt

2 tablespoons sugar

2 large eggs, beaten

3 cups buttermilk

1 teaspoon pure vanilla extract

Unsalted butter, for cooking and serving

2 cups fresh blueberries

2 ripe bananas, thinly sliced

Pure maple syrup, for serving

Place the flour, baking powder, salt, and sugar in a large bowl and whisk together. Add the eggs, buttermilk, and vanilla and whisk just until combined (a few lumps are okay, and it's better to leave them than whisk the batter too much).

Place a griddle or a large nonstick skillet over medium heat. Coat the surface of the griddle or skillet with butter (about 1 teaspoon) and ladle the batter onto the surface, making whatever size pancakes you like. Put a few blueberries and banana slices on each pancake and cook until the undersides are golden brown and small bubbles appear on top around the fruit, 1 to 2 minutes, then carefully flip each pancake over. Cook until golden on the bottom, about 1 minute. Repeat, being sure to butter the griddle or skillet between each batch, until you run out of batter.

Serve the pancakes warm, with whatever blueberries and bananas are left, plus extra butter and maple syrup.

Best-Ever French Toast

Incredibly crunchy on the outside (thanks to cornflakes!) and soft within, this is the ultimate French toast. Just like with the pancakes on page 27, if you don't have a griddle and can't make more than a couple of slices of French toast at the same time, keep the finished ones warm in a 250°F oven while you cook the rest of the batch. This French toast is really nice served with jam instead of, or in addition to, maple syrup. A little fresh fruit, like sliced oranges with mint leaves, makes for a complete meal. Eat while still in your pajamas.

4 large eggs, beaten

1¼ cups whole milk

2 tablespoons pure maple syrup, plus more for serving

1 teaspoon pure vanilla extract

2 cups finely crushed cornflakes

8 thick slices brioche or challah bread

Unsalted butter, for cooking and serving

Place the eggs, milk, maple syrup, and vanilla in a large, shallow bowl (or a baking dish) and whisk together. Place the cornflakes in another large shallow bowl.

Working with one slice of bread at a time, dip the bread into the egg mixture just to coat it on both sides (don't let it soak) and then dredge it in the cornflakes, being sure each side is coated evenly (don't pat the cereal into the bread).

Place a griddle pan or a large nonstick skillet over medium heat. Generously coat the surface of the griddle or skillet with butter (about 1 tablespoon) and add as many slices of French toast as will fit comfortably in a single layer. Cook the French toast until golden brown on the bottom, about 2 minutes. Flip each slice and cook until golden on the second side, 1 to 2 minutes. Repeat with remaining slices, being sure to butter the griddle or skillet between each batch.

Serve the French toast warm, with extra butter and maple syrup.

Our Breakfast Potatoes

We make tons (literally) of these at all our resorts, so you could say we know our way around a breakfast potato. The trick is boiling the potatoes first before crisping them in a hot skillet so that they're tender inside. We combine them with peppers, onions, and herbs to add extra flavor and color. Serve these with eggs and bacon for a classic American breakfast. They're also good for a side dish any time of day, especially alongside roast chicken or grilled sausages.

Kosher salt

1¼ pounds Yukon Gold potatoes, cut into bite-size pieces

2 tablespoons neutral oil (such as canola or vegetable)

2 tablespoons unsalted butter

½ small red bell pepper, finely diced

½ small green bell pepper, finely diced

1 small yellow onion, finely diced

2 garlic cloves, minced

1 teaspoon minced fresh thyme leaves

1 teaspoon minced fresh rosemary leaves

Small handful of fresh parsley leaves, coarsely chopped

Large pinch of flaky sea salt (or additional kosher salt), for serving

Bring a large pot of salted water to a boil. Add the potatoes and cook until barely tender, about 10 minutes. Drain the potatoes in a colander and shake them to make sure they're really dry. Let the potatoes sit in the colander for about 2 minutes to let any excess water drain.

Place the oil and butter in a large nonstick skillet set over medium-high heat. Add the drained potatoes, bell peppers, onion, garlic, thyme, rosemary, and a large pinch of kosher salt. Cook, stirring now and then (but not too much, because you want the potatoes to crisp), until the vegetables are softened and browned and the potatoes are a little bit crisp, about 15 minutes.

Sprinkle with the parsley and flaky salt and serve immediately.

Appetizers

"SMELL THOSE SHRIMP— THEY'RE BEGINNIN' TO BOIL...."

We love nothing more than gathering friends around our tables and giving them everything they need to have a great time. Since appetizers are the first impression our food makes, we're obsessed with them. Whether it's a pile of crispy, spicy chicken wings to keep your cold beer company while you're watching a game with your pals or a big pile of Peel-and-Eat Shrimp (page 41) enjoyed outside with a view of the water they came from, we've got you covered. From our world famous Volcano Nachos (page 36) to our Warm Asiago Crab Dip (page 39), we love coming up with fun dishes that everyone can share and enjoy. This chapter includes a really eclectic mix of food from all our locations. There are old-fashioned favorites and new classics like Crispy Calamari with Peppadews and Lemon Aioli (page 57). No matter if you're gearing up for a celebratory meal with JWB Crab and Quinoa Cakes with Curry Kale Slaw (page 54) as the kickoff or serving kids a pile of Cajun Chicken Quesadillas (page 91), all of our favorite appetizers are now yours.

Volcano Nachos

"I don't know where I'm a-gonna go when the volcano blow!"

We don't like to brag, but our nachos are unrivaled (and are the most photographed item at our restaurants). The secret is not much of a secret: they're so good because we make each component from scratch, and cheese and chili are on each and every bite. While we take a lot of pride in using real, whole foods in everything, we make a special exception for Velveeta in the cheese sauce here. Nothing melts like it. Nothing. In our restaurants, we build the nachos in a mixing bowl, and we make sure each and every location uses the same size bowl so that the nachos are consistent no matter where you eat them. When we invert the nachos, they take on the shape of a volcano, complete with melted cheese sauce acting as the most delicious lava. We've given those instructions here, but if you prefer to just layer them on a large baking sheet or a large platter so that you have more surface area, that works, too.

1 cup coarsely grated cheddar cheese

8 ounces Velveeta cheese, diced

¼ cup whole milk

¼ cup Ro*Tel Original diced tomatoes and green chiles,
strained Pico de Gallo (page 238), or your favorite salsa

One 10-ounce bag tortilla chips (preferably Margaritaville Restaurant-Style Tortilla chips)

2 cups Best-Ever Chili (page 164), warm

1 cup Pico de Gallo (page 238)

Sour cream, Guacamole (page 241), pickled jalapeños, and fresh cilantro for serving

Preheat the broiler to high. Position the oven rack so it's 12 inches away from the heating element.

Place the cheddar, Velveeta, milk, and Ro*Tel tomatoes and chiles in a saucepan set over medium heat. Cook, stirring, until all the cheese has melted and the sauce is smooth, about 3 minutes. Keep the sauce warm over low heat.

Place an even, single layer of chips on the bottom of a large bowl. Drizzle with a little cheese sauce, spoon over some of the warm chili, and top with some of the pico de gallo. Repeat the process until you've used up all the sauce, chili, and pico de gallo. Place a large broiler-safe serving bowl or platter (anything with a larger diameter than the bowl) over the bowl and quickly, assertively, and safely invert the nachos onto it. They will be messy, but that's the point! Place the platter under the broiler and cook until the cheese sauce and chili are bubbling, about 3 minutes. Top the nachos with sour cream, guacamole, pickled jalapeños, and cilantro. Serve immediately.

Warm Asiago Crab Dip

One of the most popular appetizers at Margaritaville, this warm crab dip is full of cheese and marinated artichoke hearts. We serve ours with thin rounds of crostini (toasted bread), but you could also use crackers, tortilla chips, celery sticks, or endive leaves. This is good to serve for a party because you can assemble the dip in its baking dish and refrigerate it for up to two days before baking.

One 8-ounce package cream cheese, at room temperature

1 cup mayonnaise

1 cup sour cream

2 tablespoons fresh lemon juice

1 teaspoon hot sauce

1 teaspoon Worcestershire sauce

1 tablespoon Margaritaville House Spice Blend (page 128)

1½ cups finely grated Asiago cheese

1 cup coarsely grated Monterey Jack cheese

1 cup marinated, drained artichoke hearts, rinsed and finely chopped

2 tablespoons finely chopped fresh parsley

1 pound fresh or pasteurized crab claw meat

½ cup panko bread crumbs

1 tablespoon neutral oil (such as canola or vegetable)

Small handful of fresh chives, minced

Zest of 1 small lemon, thinly sliced

Crostini, for serving

Preheat the oven to 400°F.

Place the cream cheese, mayonnaise, sour cream, lemon juice, hot sauce, Worcestershire, and Margaritaville House Spice Blend in a food processor and puree until well combined.

Add 1 cup of the Asiago, the Monterey Jack, artichoke hearts, and parsley. Pulse until well combined (but not too smooth, just combined).

Transfer the mixture to a large bowl and gently fold in the crabmeat. Transfer the dip to a shallow baking dish (a pie dish works well).

Place the remaining ½ cup Asiago in a small bowl. Add the panko and the oil and stir well to combine. Sprinkle the mixture evenly over the crab dip.

Bake until the bread crumbs are golden brown and the dip is bubbling, about 15 minutes.

Sprinkle the chives and lemon zest over the dip and serve warm with crostini.

Grilled Oysters with Tarragon Butter

Serves 4

These oysters are best enjoyed on the beach around a fire built from driftwood. If you do that, make the tarragon butter at home and just bring it with you in a jar. You can also of course successfully make these at home on an outdoor grill (gas or charcoal—both work) or under the intense heat of the broiler. You can also substitute a bourbon-chipotle butter for the tarragon butter (simply mix 1 minced chipotle pepper and a splash of bourbon into the butter).

4 tablespoons (½ stick) unsalted butter, at room temperature

½ teaspoon kosher salt

½ teaspoon freshly ground black pepper

1 teaspoon minced fresh tarragon

½ teaspoon minced fresh marjoram

½ teaspoon white wine vinegar

12 fresh oysters

1 lemon, cut into wedges, for serving

Preheat an outdoor grill to high.

Place the butter, salt, pepper, tarragon, marjoram, and vinegar in a small bowl and use a fork to mix everything together.

Place the oysters on the hot grill, rounded-side down, and cook until they pop open, about 3 minutes. Carefully remove the oysters from the grill and pry off and discard the top shells. Divide the butter among the hot oysters so it can melt directly on top of the oysters. Serve immediately, with lemon wedges for squeezing over.

Peel-and-Eat Shrimp

Serves 4

Originally featured on the menu at our first café in Key West, we began serving these to celebrate Key West's "pinks" shrimp. Use the freshest shrimp you can find and share with friends who don't mind getting their hands messy. Serve for a group that has lots to catch up on, since peeling the shrimp gives you a perfect activity to pass the time.

2 ½ cups beer (preferably LandShark Lager)

2 tablespoons Old Bay Seasoning

2 lemons, halved crosswise

1 ½ pounds shell-on medium shrimp, deveined (but leave shells on)

½ cup Mustard Sauce (recipe follows), for serving

Large pinch of dried red chile flakes, for serving (optional)

1 small handful of fresh parsley stems, for serving (optional)

Place the beer, Old Bay, and 2 of the lemon halves (1 whole lemon) in a large pot set over high heat. Bring the mixture to a boil, add the shrimp, and turn off the heat. Cover the pot and let the shrimp cook in the hot beer until firm to the touch and opaque, 5 minutes.

Drain the shrimp in a colander (discard the lemon halves and cooking liquid or save it for another use, such as making chowder). Transfer shrimp to a serving platter. Place the remaining lemon halves on the platter. Place the mustard sauce in a small bowl and sprinkle with the chile flakes (if using). Decorate the platter with the parsley (if using) and serve immediately while the shrimp are warm, with an empty bowl for shells and plenty of napkins.

Mustard Sauce

Not only is this sauce for dipping the shrimp into, it's also excellent on stone crab claws, if you can find them! It's even wonderful on a turkey sandwich.

½ cup mayonnaise

1 tablespoon Dijon mustard

1 tablespoon sour cream

½ teaspoon Worcestershire sauce

½ teaspoon A.1. Steak Sauce

Pinch of kosher salt

Place all the ingredients in a small bowl and whisk together. Serve immediately or store in an airtight container in the fridge for up to 1 week.

Drunken Shrimp Skillet

To earn the title, we put a small splash of silver tequila in the garlicky butter that adorns these shrimp, but feel free to use a generous pour if you prefer a bit more (or leave it out and just call it "Buttery Shrimp Skillet"). For a full meal, toss the shrimp with a pound of cooked spaghetti and add a few handfuls of baby spinach.

6 tablespoons (¾ stick) unsalted butter, melted

2 tablespoons silver tequila (preferably Margaritaville Silver Tequila)

1 tablespoon key lime juice (preferably Nellie & Joe's) or fresh lime juice

1 scallion, thinly sliced

3 garlic cloves, minced

½ teaspoon kosher salt

½ teaspoon freshly ground black pepper

2 tablespoons olive oil

1 small red onion, thinly sliced

1 small red bell pepper, thinly sliced

1 small yellow bell pepper, thinly sliced

1 small green bell pepper, thinly sliced

1 pound medium shrimp, peeled and deveined

4 thick slices bread, toasted, for serving

Place the butter, tequila, lime juice, scallion, one-third of the minced garlic, the salt, and the black pepper in a small bowl and whisk together. Set aside.

Place the olive oil in a large skillet set over medium-high heat. Once it's hot, add the remaining minced garlic and the onion and bell peppers and cook, stirring now and then, until the peppers are softened and browned in spots, about 8 minutes. Add the shrimp and cook, stirring so they cook evenly on both sides, until firm to the touch and opaque, about 1½ minutes per side. Add the butter mixture and cook, stirring, just until it melts.

Serve the shrimp immediately, straight out of the skillet, with toasted bread for dipping.

Lava Lava Shrimp

Hot, crispy fried shrimp need no ornament, but we think they are best served on a bed of cool iceberg lettuce and drizzled with a spicy sauce full of flavors like key lime juice, soy sauce, and garlic. These could also be served as tacos (substitute shredded green cabbage for the lettuce and pile everything in soft corn tortillas).

FOR THE SAUCE

½ cup mayonnaise

½ teaspoon chile oil

¼ teaspoon toasted sesame oil

1 tablespoon soy sauce

1 small garlic clove, minced

2 tablespoons key lime juice (preferably Nellie & Joe's) or fresh lime juice

2 tablespoons chile sauce (preferably Sriracha)

1 teaspoon togarashi (Japanese pepper mix) or freshly ground black pepper

FOR THE SHRIMP

½ cup buttermilk

1 teaspoon kosher salt

1 pound medium shrimp, peeled and deveined

¼ cup cornmeal

¼ cup all-purpose flour

½ teaspoon baking soda

⅔ cup ice-cold sparkling water

Neutral oil (such as canola or vegetable), for frying

TO SERVE

½ head iceberg lettuce, shredded

MAKE THE SAUCE: Place the mayonnaise, chile oil, sesame oil, soy sauce, garlic, key lime juice, chile sauce, togarashi, and 3 tablespoons water in a small bowl. Whisk together and set aside.

PREPARE THE SHRIMP: Place the buttermilk and $1/2$ teaspoon of the salt in a medium bowl and whisk together. Add the shrimp and stir to combine.

In a separate bowl, whisk together the cornmeal, flour, baking soda, and remaining $1/2$ teaspoon salt. Whisk in the sparkling water.

Pour 1 inch of oil into a large heavy pot and heat the oil over medium heat. Test the oil: When a pinch of the batter sizzles upon contact, it's ready. Drain the shrimp (discard the buttermilk) and coat them in the batter. Carefully place them into the hot oil, working in batches as necessary so the shrimp don't crowd the pot. Cook, turning the shrimp a few times as they cook, until golden brown all over, about 4 minutes. Transfer the fried shrimp to a paper towel–lined plate to drain while you cook the remaining shrimp.

ASSEMBLE AND SERVE: Spread the lettuce over the surface of a serving platter and top with the hot fried shrimp. Place the sauce in a small serving bowl and serve immediately.

Conch Fritters with Calypso Sauce

Serves 4

Completely addictive, these fritters are inspired by the Bahamian ones served at Herbie's Bar & Chowder House, the oldest operating restaurant in Marathon, Florida, which happens to be the exact halfway point between Key Largo and Key West. The batter is filled not only with a generous amount of conch, but also flavors like thyme, fresh onion, and pepper. The most surprising ingredient in the batter is ketchup, which lends sweetness and color to the fritters. If you can't track down conch, you can substitute an equal amount of chopped raw shrimp. If you track down too much conch and have extra, consider making a pot of our Bahamian Conch Chowder (page 119).

1 cup all-purpose flour

1 teaspoon baking powder

1 teaspoon kosher salt

½ teaspoon red pepper flakes

½ teaspoon dried thyme

½ cup ketchup

½ small yellow onion, finely diced

½ green bell pepper, finely diced

1 cup conch (drained if canned or thawed and drained if frozen), finely chopped

Neutral oil (such as canola or vegetable), for frying

1 cup Calypso Sauce (recipe follows), for serving

Small handful of fresh parsley leaves, for serving

Place the flour, baking powder, salt, red pepper flakes, and thyme in a large bowl and whisk well to combine. Add the ketchup, onion, bell pepper, and ¼ cup water and stir until everything is evenly combined. Fold in the conch.

Pour 1 inch of oil into a large heavy pot and heat the oil over medium heat. Test the oil: When a pinch of the batter sizzles upon contact, it's ready. Scoop golf ball–size portions of the batter into the hot oil, working in batches as necessary so the fritters don't crowd the pot. Cook, turning the fritters a few times while they cook, until browned all over, about 5 minutes. Transfer the fritters to a paper towel–lined plate and continue frying until you've used up all your batter.

Serve the fritters hot sprinkled with parsley leaves, with the Calypso Sauce on the side.

Calypso Sauce

Our version of Russian dressing, we spike the classic combination of ketchup and mayonnaise with a little yellow mustard and a lot of coconut rum. For kids or anyone else not interested in spiked sauce, feel free to leave out the rum.

½ cup ketchup

¼ cup mayonnaise

2 teaspoons yellow mustard

2 tablespoons coconut rum

Place all the ingredients in a large bowl and whisk together. Serve immediately or store in an airtight container in the fridge for up to 1 week.

Spanish Octopus Salad

Serves 6

One of Spain's most well-known and beloved tapas dishes, this octopus salad hails from Galicia, the northwest corner of Spain, where octopus has been prepared for centuries. Carlo had it for the first time there after walking the final twelve hours of the Camino de Santiago (also known as the Way of St. James) pilgrimage. He found a tavern where older women spent all day poaching octopus in 40-gallon copper pots. He ate and drank Albariño wine for hours and then finished his walk to the Santiago de Compostela cathedral. As Carlo says, "Simple, traditional ways to cook are the ones that hold for generations and will always be in peoples' memories." Carlo learned the unusual method of rubbing the octopus with salt and then poaching it in water mixed with gluten-free soy sauce and black tea from chef Kon Lee, who is the mastermind behind the sushi at JWB. It helps keep the octopus incredibly tender and adds extra flavor. See the note at the end of the recipe if you prefer a more Mediterranean cooking method.

4 cups gluten-free soy sauce

1 black tea bag

Kosher salt

One 3-pound octopus, brain removed

12 large Yukon Gold potatoes

2 celery stalks (including leaves), diced

¼ cup extra-virgin olive oil

2 teaspoons pimentón (Spanish smoked sweet paprika)

Place the soy sauce, tea bag, 1 tablespoon kosher salt, and 2 gallons water in a large lobster pot or canning pot (or a large copper pot if you have one, as per Spanish tradition). Set the pot over high heat and bring the water to a boil, then reduce the heat to low to keep the water at a very gentle simmer. If you have one, use a digital thermometer to gauge the temperature and regulate the heat so that water remains 166°F.

Meanwhile, rub the octopus vigorously with 2 cups salt so that it creates a foamlike effect. Wipe the octopus clean with paper towels. Holding the octopus by its head, dip it in the simmering water and then pull it back out. Repeat the process three more times and drop it in the water on the fourth dip (this is a Spanish custom Carlo picked up and helps to warm the octopus). Cook the octopus for 10 minutes and then, transfer it to a large bowl. Let the octopus cool for 30 minutes.

(continued)

Meanwhile, bring a large pot of water to a boil and salt it generously. Add the potatoes and cook until they're just tender when pierced with a paring knife, about 18 minutes. Transfer the potatoes to a cutting board. Once they're cool enough to handle, peel them and cut them into $\frac{1}{4}$-inch-thick slices. Place the sliced potatoes on a large serving platter and sprinkle them with a large pinch of salt.

Cut the cooled octopus into 1-inch pieces and place them in a bowl with the celery, olive oil, and paprika. Mix well to combine. Taste the octopus and season with salt if needed (it probably won't need any).

Place the dressed octopus on top of the potatoes. Serve immediately.

Note: If you prefer a more traditionally Mediterranean cooking method, use the same large pot and fill it with 3 gallons water with enough salt to make it taste lightly salted, 1 cup white wine, a few whole black peppercorns, a dried bay leaf, a wine cork, and a 3-inch piece of food-safe copper pipe (which you can find at the hardware store). The cork and copper pipe will help keep the octopus tender (and if you can't track down the pipe, simply omit it). Set the pot over high heat and bring the water to a boil. Rub the octopus with the salt just as described in the method and plunge it into the boiling water three times, then release it into the water on the fourth. Reduce the heat to maintain a simmer and cook until the octopus is tender but still has a little bite (like cooking pasta al dente), 20 to 25 minutes, depending on the size of the octopus. Continue with the recipe as described.

Octopus Tiradito: **For an entirely different recipe within this same one, cook the octopus as directed. Whisk together $\frac{1}{2}$ cup mayonnaise, 2 tablespoons fresh lime juice, 2 tablespoons chile paste (preferably ají amarillo chile paste), and $\frac{1}{2}$ teaspoon kosher salt. Cut the octopus into thin pieces, place them on a serving platter, and drizzle with the mayonnaise mixture. Top with finely chopped fresh cilantro and thinly sliced red onion.**

JWB Crab and Quinoa Cakes with Curry Kale Slaw

Serves 4

These crab cakes are just barely bound with quinoa and chickpeas, which allow us to forgo the usual bread crumbs and eggs. This mixture makes the crab cakes much healthier and also more interesting. The vibrant Curry Kale Slaw, which perfectly complements the crab's sweetness, also really sets these apart. You can serve these with extra dressing from the slaw or even a bit of Mustard Sauce (page 42). You can also serve them as sandwiches, or even throw in a little bacon for an elevated crab cake BLT!

¼ cup minced red onion

¼ cup minced red bell pepper

¼ cup minced yellow bell pepper

1 cup cooked quinoa

1¼ cups canned chickpeas, drained and rinsed

¼ cup fresh cilantro leaves, finely chopped

½ teaspoon kosher salt

1 teaspoon freshly ground black pepper

1 tablespoon yellow curry powder

6 tablespoons fresh lemon juice

3 tablespoons olive oil

2 tablespoons Dijon mustard

1 pound fresh or pasteurized jumbo lump crabmeat

2 tablespoons neutral oil (such as canola or vegetable), for frying

2 tablespoons unsalted butter, for frying

2 cups Curry Kale Slaw (recipe follows), for serving

1 lemon, cut into wedges, for serving

Place the onion, bell peppers, quinoa, chickpeas, cilantro, salt, pepper, curry powder, lemon juice, olive oil, and mustard in a food processor and pulse until well combined, about six pulses.

Line a baking sheet with parchment paper. Transfer the mixture to a large bowl and add the crab. Using clean hands, mix everything well just to combine (you don't want to overmix and break the crab apart too much). Divide the mixture into 8 equal portions and shape each one into a small patty. Place the crab cakes on the prepared baking sheet and cover with plastic wrap. Refrigerate the crab cakes for at least 1 hour and up to 24 hours before cooking.

Place 1 tablespoon of the neutral oil and 1 tablespoon of the butter in a large nonstick skillet set over medium-high heat. Once the fat is hot, add half the crab cakes in a single layer and cook until the bottoms are browned, about 2 minutes. Carefully flip the crab cakes and cook until well browned on the second side, about 2 minutes more. Transfer the crab cakes to a serving platter and repeat with the remaining oil, butter, and crab cakes.

Serve the crab cakes warm, with the Curry Kale Slaw alongside and lemon wedges for squeezing over.

Curry Kale Slaw

Not only does this slaw elevate the crab cakes on page 54, it's also the best thing to serve alongside grilled fish or chicken. The dressing for the slaw is a delicious sauce in and of itself. Try substituting it for the mayonnaise dressing on the JWB Lobster Rolls (page 155) for a completely new take on an old standby.

½ cup crème fraîche (or sour cream)

2 tablespoons plain Greek yogurt (regular or nonfat)

1½ tablespoons hot mango chutney

2 teaspoons Dijon mustard

2 teaspoons honey

1 teaspoon curry powder

½ teaspoon kosher salt

½ teaspoon freshly ground black pepper

½ pound curly kale (about ½ average bunch), tough stems discarded, leaves finely chopped

2 cups very thinly sliced red cabbage

2 cups very thinly sliced green cabbage

1 large carrot, coarsely grated

4 scallions, thinly sliced

¼ cup raisins

2 large handfuls of fresh cilantro leaves, finely chopped

Place the crème fraîche, yogurt, mango chutney, mustard, honey, curry powder, salt, and pepper in a large bowl and whisk together. Add the kale, red and green cabbage, carrot, scallions, raisins, and cilantro and stir well to combine. Serve immediately or cover and refrigerate for up to 3 days.

Crispy Calamari with Peppadews and Lemon Aioli

Fried calamari is often more about the breading than the calamari. Not ours. We coat the fresh squid with just enough batter to get it really crispy and serve it with briny, slightly spicy Peppadew peppers. Look for them in a jar in the same aisle as the pickles (they look like pickled cherry tomatoes). For a tasty sandwich, slather a toasted baguette with Lemon Aioli, top it with a big pile of crispy squid, and call it a day. Seek out calamari from Rhode Island if you can find it. . . . We think it's the best.

1½ pounds cleaned calamari (squid), tentacles separated and bodies cut into thin rings

1 cup whole milk

½ cup all-purpose flour

¼ cup plus 2 tablespoons fine cornmeal

¼ cup cornstarch

1 teaspoon kosher salt

1 teaspoon freshly ground black pepper

Neutral oil (such as canola or vegetable), for frying

½ cup drained Peppadew peppers, for serving

1 cup Lemon Aioli (recipe follows), for serving

1 lemon, cut into halves, for serving

Place the calamari and milk in a large bowl and mix well.

In a separate large bowl, place the flour, cornmeal, cornstarch, ½ teaspoon of the salt, and ½ teaspoon of the pepper and whisk together.

Lift the calamari from the milk (discard the milk) and place it into the flour mixture. Coat each piece well. Working in batches, place the dredged calamari in a small sieve and shake it over the bowl of the flour mixture to remove any excess. Set the breaded calamari aside.

Meanwhile, pour 1 inch of oil into a large heavy pot and heat the oil over medium heat. Test the oil: When a pinch of the flour mixture sizzles upon contact, it's ready. Add the calamari to the hot oil, working in batches as necessary so the calamari doesn't crowd the pot. Cook, turning the calamari a few times while they cook, until browned all over, about 3 minutes. Transfer the fried calamari to a paper towel–lined plate and cook the remaining calamari.

Place the fried calamari in a large bowl and sprinkle with the remaining ½ teaspoon salt and ½ teaspoon pepper. Toss well to combine.

Transfer the calamari to a serving platter and serve hot, with the Peppedews and aioli alongside and lemon halves for squeezing over.

Lemon Aioli

Try this homemade lemony, garlicky mayonnaise with the Crispy Calamari with Peppadews and Lemon Aioli (page 57) and honestly on just about everything else in the world. It's particularly nice as a dip for the Oven Fries (page 254). Since this includes a raw egg yolk, make sure it's pasteurized (which the US Department of Agriculture considers safe to consume). If raw egg presents a health issue for you, simply whisk the vinegar, mustard, garlic, and lemon into a cup of prepared mayonnaise.

2 teaspoons white wine vinegar

1 teaspoon Dijon mustard

1 small garlic clove, minced

Pinch of kosher salt

Pinch of freshly ground black pepper

1 large egg yolk

½ cup canola oil

¼ cup olive oil

2 teaspoons fresh lemon juice

Place the vinegar in a microwave-safe container and microwave for 15 seconds, until hot but not boiling. Set aside.

Meanwhile, place the mustard, garlic, salt, pepper, and egg yolk in a large bowl and whisk to combine. While whisking, slowly drizzle in the canola oil, drop by drop, until the mixture has emulsified. Whisk in the warm vinegar, followed by the olive oil, and finally the lemon juice. Serve immediately or store in an airtight container in the fridge for up to 2 days.

Fried Oysters with Creamed Spinach

Serves 4

Carlo started making these at JWB as a way to highlight the JWB Creamed Spinach (page 253). A mash-up of fried oysters and oysters Rockefeller, they've become one of our most popular appetizers. Serve these with a cold glass of sparkling wine! If you can find shucked, brined oysters (most fish markets have them), use those, as they're extra juicy.

1 cup buttermilk

2 tablespoons hot sauce (preferably Crystal), plus extra for serving

12 oysters, shucked, half of the shells reserved

½ cup all-purpose flour

½ cup finely ground cornmeal

1½ tablespoons cornstarch

½ teaspoon kosher salt

Neutral oil (such as canola or vegetable), for frying

1½ cups JWB Creamed Spinach (page 253), warmed

Place the buttermilk and hot sauce in a medium-size bowl and whisk together. Add the oysters and stir to combine. Cover the bowl and refrigerate for at least 3 hours and up to 6 hours.

Place the flour, cornmeal, cornstarch, and salt in a separate medium bowl and whisk together.

Lift the oysters from the buttermilk (discard the buttermilk) and place them in the flour mixture. Coat each oyster well. Working in batches, place the dredged oysters in a small sieve and shake over the bowl of flour mixture to remove any excess. Set the oysters aside.

Meanwhile, pour 1 inch of oil into a large heavy pot and heat the oil over medium heat. Test the oil: When a pinch of the flour mixture sizzles upon contact, it's ready. Add the dredged oysters to the hot oil, working in batches as necessary so the oysters don't crowd the pot. Cook, turning the oysters a few times while they cook, until browned all over, about 3 minutes. Transfer the fried oysters to a paper towel–lined plate and cook the remaining oysters.

Place 2 tablespoons of the warm JWB Creamed Spinach on each reserved oyster shell and top each one with a fried oyster. Put a dash of hot sauce on each oyster. Serve immediately.

Lionfish Carpaccio

Carlo says best to make this when you've been spearfishing all day and get back on your boat and realize you haven't eaten anything and you barely have any provisions. Spearfishing not only yields better-tasting food on your plate (because the fish don't release lactic acid as they do when caught with a rod and reel), but helps protect the ecosystem. Lionfish tastes simple, fresh, and mild. When you eat it, you are doing a service to the environment: it's an invasive species that Carlo and his team are at the forefront of the efforts to control.

1 pound fresh lionfish

3 tablespoons olive oil

3 tablespoons fresh lemon juice

Kosher salt

Freshly ground black pepper

2 tablespoons drained brined capers

Large handful of fresh arugula or watercress

Clean and gut your fish if you haven't already. When fish is this fresh, it will be extra warm and buttery. To cut it on as wide an angle as possible, place the fish in the freezer for 20 minutes (throw a plate in there, too). This will make it much easier to cut the fish very thinly without ripping it. Thinly slice the fish and place the slices on the cold plate (the plate helps keep the fish cold!).

Drizzle the olive oil and lemon juice over the fish and sprinkle lightly with salt and pepper. Top with the capers and arugula. Enjoy immediately.

A Day on a Boat

Kusshi Oysters with Granny Smith, Cucumber, and Mint Granita

Serves 4

A perfect happy-hour snack, these refreshing oysters are amazing on a hot day. We like Kusshis, small oysters from the Pacific Northwest, since they're sweet and mild. Use whatever type you like and is available near you. Serve these on a bed of rock salt or crushed ice to keep them steady.

1 Granny Smith apple, peeled, cored, and coarsely chopped

1 medium cucumber, peeled, seeded, and coarsely chopped

4 large fresh mint leaves

2 tablespoons sugar

2 tablespoons fresh lemon juice

12 Kusshi oysters or your preferred oysters

Small handful of fresh dill, coarsely chopped

Place the apple, cucumber, mint, sugar, and lemon juice in a blender. Shuck the oysters and pour their juices into the blender. Put the oysters in a small bowl and their shells in a separate medium bowl, cover both, and refrigerate.

Puree the apple mixture until smooth and then transfer to a shallow container or baking dish. Freeze the mixture until icy, about 40 minutes. Scrape it with a fork and return it to the freezer. Scrape the granita every 15 minutes or so until it is flaky and frozen, about 2 ½ hours total.

Place the oysters back in their shells and spoon the granita on top of the shucked oysters and top each one with a little bit of dill. Serve immediately.

Veracruz Seafood Cocktail

You will need the contents of basically the entire fish market for this seafood cocktail. Use whatever is available in the store, as long as it's fresh—get whatever selection of fish and shellfish looks best and feel free to mix and match. Quickly poached shrimp and calamari get mixed with plenty of raw oysters and clams. Combined with tomatoes in various forms (raw, ketchup, and juice!), cilantro, and plenty of chiles, this is a true cocktail in that all the various parts come together to create an incredible whole. This dish, known in some areas as a hangover cure, is based on the iconic food served by fishermen all over the coastal towns of Central and South America, including Veracruz, Mexico. Best enjoyed with a view of the water the seafood just came out of.

1 pound large shrimp, peeled and deveined

1 pound cleaned calamari (squid), tentacles separated and halved, bodies cut into thin rings

½ cup fresh lime juice

1 pound plum tomatoes, cored, seeded, finely chopped

1 cup ketchup

1 teaspoon hot sauce (preferably Tabasco)

1 cup tomato juice (preferably V8)

1 cup finely chopped fresh cilantro

½ cup finely chopped fresh parsley

¼ cup Worcestershire sauce

¼ cup plus 2 tablespoons olive oil

2 fresh serrano peppers or jalapeños, thinly sliced

1 medium white onion, finely diced

18 small oysters, shucked, juices reserved

18 small clams, shucked, juices reserved

Kosher salt

2 ripe avocados, pitted, peeled, and thinly sliced

Saltine crackers, for serving

Place 8 cups water in a large pot set over high heat. Bring the water to a boil and add the shrimp. Cook, stirring, until pink and just firm to the touch, about 2 minutes. Use a slotted spoon to transfer the shrimp to a cutting board and let cool. Add the calamari to the pot and cook, stirring, until just cooked through and opaque, about 1 minute. Drain the calamari in a colander. Cut the shrimp into 1-inch pieces and transfer them to a bowl. Add the calamari to the bowl along with the lime juice, tomatoes, ketchup, hot sauce, tomato juice, cilantro, parsley, Worcestershire, olive oil, chiles, onion, and the oysters and clams along with their juices. Gently fold everything together. Season the mixture to taste with salt. Transfer the seafood to glass goblets or bowls and top with the avocado. Serve immediately with crackers on the side.

Tuna Poke with Plantain Chips

Serves 4

Tuna poke (po-kay) is a lot like tuna tartare but with all the flavors of traditional Hawaiian poke, including lots of fresh ginger. It's an easy but very elegant first course and goes especially well with festive drinks like Frozen Paradise Palomas (page 311). For a vegan version, substitute small cubes of watermelon for the tuna and leave the honey out.

1 pound fresh sushi-grade ahi tuna loin, in one whole piece

6 scallions, thinly sliced

1 garlic clove, minced

¼ cup minced fresh ginger

½ medium cucumber, seeded and finely diced

Large handful of fresh cilantro leaves, minced

2 tablespoons fresh orange juice

1½ tablespoons Japanese ponzu sauce (or fresh lime juice)

1½ teaspoons toasted sesame oil

1½ teaspoons honey

1½ teaspoons chile paste (preferably Sambal Oelek)

1 teaspoon wasabi paste

1 teaspoon kosher salt, plus more as needed

1 ripe avocado, pitted, peeled, and diced

1 tablespoon fresh lime juice

2 teaspoons toasted sesame seeds

1 recipe Plantain Chips (recipe follows), for serving

Roll the tuna tightly in plastic wrap and place it in the freezer for 2 hours so that the exterior is firm, but it's not frozen to the core. Unwrap it and use the sharpest knife you have to cut it into ½-inch cubes. Place the tuna in a large bowl and add the scallions, garlic, ginger, cucumber, cilantro, orange juice, ponzu, sesame oil, honey, chile paste, wasabi paste, and salt. Gently stir everything together. Taste and season with salt if needed and transfer it to the center of a serving dish. Top with the avocado and drizzle the avocado with the lime juice. Sprinkle the sesame seeds on top. Surround with the plantain chips for scooping. Serve immediately.

Plantain Chips

Essential as vehicles for our Tuna Poke (page 71), these chips are also, in and of themselves, a delicious snack. Serve them with cocktails instead of regular old potato chips or pack them in a container to bring on the boat with Cuban Meat Loaf Survival Sandwiches (page 140).

2 green plantains, peeled

Neutral oil (such as canola or vegetable), for frying

Kosher salt

Use a sharp knife or a mandoline to slice the plantains into ⅛-inch-thick strips.

Pour 1 inch of oil into a large pot and heat the oil over medium-high heat. Test the oil: When a piece of plantain sizzles upon contact, it's ready. Add the plantain strips to the oil, working in batches as necessary to avoid crowding, and fry, turning the pieces now and then, until golden brown all over and crunchy, about 1 minute. Transfer the plantains to a paper towel–lined plate to drain and sprinkle with a large pinch of salt. Serve at room temperature.

Paradise Ceviche

Serves 4

Carlo spent a lot of time living and cooking in South America and has introduced us to so many techniques and flavors that he picked up along the way. The ceviche is a classic Peruvian dish that's all about the freshest fish, one of Carlo's passions. Be sure to only make this if you can get incredibly high-quality fish. If you can't find *cancha* (Peruvian fried corn), you can substitute corn nuts, and if you can't find choclo (Peruvian corn kernels), you can substitute drained and rinsed canned hominy.

1½ pounds high-quality firm, white-fleshed fish (such as grouper or snapper), cut into 1-inch cubes

½ teaspoon kosher salt

1 tablespoon bonito flakes

1½ teaspoons minced fresh aji limo chile (or any hot pepper, such as jalapeño or habanero)

1 garlic clove, minced

1½ cups fresh lime juice (from about 12 limes)

1 small red onion, thinly sliced

Small handful of fresh cilantro, finely chopped

¼ cup cancha (Peruvian fried corn)

¼ cup choclo (Peruvian corn kernels)

Place the fish in a large bowl set over an even larger bowl of crushed ice (this will keep the fish nice and cold while you prepare it).

Sprinkle the salt, bonito flakes, chile, and garlic over the fish and stir to combine. Add the lime juice, onion, and cilantro and gently mix. Let the fish sit for a minute to marinate. Divide the fish and all the juice from the bowl among four serving glasses or bowls and evenly divide the cancha and choclo among them. Serve immediately.

Belizean Shrimp Ceviche

When we opened LandShark Bar & Grill in Harvest Caye, Belize, we tried so many different types of shrimp ceviche all over the coastal town of Placencia (where you catch the ferry to Harvest Caye). This version is the way we serve it, and it's perfect for anyone wary of raw seafood, since the shrimp are poached first. We love serving this in a plantain nest, which is easy to do at the restaurant with a deep fryer. To make them at home requires some ambition, but is entirely doable—see the note below for instructions. You can also just serve the ceviche in glasses or bowls with store-bought plantain chips or tortilla chips on top.

1 tablespoon kosher salt, plus more as needed

1 tablespoon freshly ground black pepper, plus more as needed

1 lemon, halved

2 dried bay leaves

1 pound medium shrimp, peeled and deveined

½ cup Pico de Gallo (page 238)

1 tablespoon minced jalapeño

½ cup fresh lemon juice

¼ cup finely diced bell pepper (any color)

¼ cup finely diced red onion

Fill a large pot with water and add the salt, black pepper, lemon halves, and bay leaves and bring it to a boil. Lower the heat to a simmer and add the shrimp and cook, stirring, until they're just opaque, about 2 minutes. Drain the shrimp and rinse them with cool running water (discard the lemon halves and bay leaves). Coarsely chop the shrimp and place them in a large bowl. Add the pico de gallo, jalapeño, lemon juice, bell pepper, and onion and mix well to combine. Season with salt and black pepper and then chill until super cold. This can sit in the fridge for up to 2 days and will just get more flavorful, almost like Southern pickled shrimp. Serve cold in glasses or bowls.

To make a plantain nest: Coarsely grate peeled green plantains and then dry the shreds on a kitchen towel and season well with salt. Place a handful of the shredded plantains in a small chinois (a conical strainer) and spread them so the shreds form an even layer up the sides of the strainer. Place another chinois on top so that the plantains are sandwiched between them and plunge the whole thing into a vat of oil. Cook until golden brown and crispy, about 5 minutes. Carefully remove the nest from the chinois and drain on a paper towel.

Pimiento Cheese Hushpuppies

Hushpuppies are basically bite-size fritters made of cornmeal batter. They get their name because it's been said that cooks back in the day would fry off some batter and throw the fritters to the dogs to get them to hush. Lucky dogs! We put our homemade Pimiento Cheese not only in the hushpuppies, but also alongside of them for a fully Southern treat. These are lovely with cocktails in the evening or served alongside LandShark Beer–Battered Fish (page 217) with Cilantro-Lime Coleslaw (page 242). Look for pimiento peppers in jars near the pickles in the grocery store.

¾ cup plus 2 tablespoons cornmeal

½ cup plus 1 tablespoon all-purpose flour

2½ teaspoons baking powder

2 teaspoons baking soda

2 teaspoons sugar

2 teaspoons kosher salt

½ teaspoon freshly ground black pepper

¼ cup plus 2 tablespoons beer (preferably LandShark Lager)

1 large egg, beaten

3 scallions, minced

3 tablespoons drained pimiento peppers

⅓ cup coarsely grated sharp white cheddar cheese

1 recipe Pimiento Cheese (recipe follows)

Neutral oil (such as canola or vegetable), for frying

Place the cornmeal, flour, baking powder, baking soda, sugar, salt, and pepper in a large bowl and whisk together.

Place the beer and egg in a separate bowl and whisk together until frothy. Stir in the scallions, pimientos, cheddar, and 1 tablespoon of the pimiento cheese.

Stir the beer mixture into the cornmeal mixture. Cover the mixture and refrigerate for at least 1 hour and up to 24 hours.

Pour 1 inch of oil into a large heavy pot and heat the oil over medium-high heat. Test the oil: When a pinch of the batter sizzles upon contact, it's ready. Scoop golf ball–size portions of the batter into the oil, working in batches as necessary so that the hushpuppies don't crowd the pot. Cook, turning the hushpuppies a few times while they cook, until browned all over, about 3 minutes. Transfer the hushpuppies to a paper towel-lined plate and continue frying until you've used up all the batter.

Serve hot, with the remaining pimiento cheese alongside.

Pimiento Cheese

Makes about 1 cup

We love putting this traditional pimiento cheese not just in the hushpuppies on page 77, but also serving a bowl of it alongside of them. When you spread a little on a hot hushpuppy, it melts and makes for the most delicious bite ever. Our pimiento cheese has a bit of heat from a jarred pickled jalapeño. We have whole ones in our kitchens, but if you have a jar of sliced ones, simply chop up about a dozen slices and you'll be good to go. We also like the texture of this to be rustic, but if you prefer yours a bit smoother, simply place everything in a food processor and pulse it instead of just stirring it together in a bowl.

¾ cup coarsely grated sharp yellow cheddar cheese

¾ cup drained pimiento peppers, finely chopped

1 whole pickled jalapeño, finely chopped

¼ teaspoon kosher salt

¼ teaspoon cayenne pepper

½ cup mayonnaise

Place everything in a bowl and stir it together. That's that!

Crispy Eggplant and Goat Cheese— Stuffed Piquillo Peppers

Serves 4

Once you track down a jar of piquillos (Spanish roasted peppers), you're good to go for this simple dish. Look for them in the international aisle of the grocery store or on tienda.com. Serve as an appetizer on a big platter of baby arugula dressed with lemon and olive oil, or serve as a nosh to have with a cocktail or a glass of Red Wine and Cherry Sangria (page 314) or White Wine and Peach Sangria (page 314). Warming the peppers with garlic and a pinch of sugar gives them so much extra flavor and should not be skipped.

Olive oil

2 small garlic cloves, minced

8 jarred piquillo peppers, drained

1 teaspoon coarse sugar (preferably turbinado) or granulated sugar

1 eggplant, cut into thin rounds

Kosher salt

2 large eggs, beaten

1 cup fine bread crumbs

4 ounces plain goat cheese, at room temperature

Small handful of microgreens (or fresh parsley leaves), for serving

Place 2 tablespoons olive oil in a medium skillet set over medium heat. Add the garlic and once it begins to sizzle and smell fragrant, add the peppers. Sprinkle with the sugar and cook, turning the peppers now and then, until they're warm and fragrant, about 2 minutes. Turn off the heat and transfer the peppers and their cooking juices to a large plate. Let them cool to room temperature and then cover and refrigerate until cold, at least 1 hour or up to overnight.

While the peppers are cooling, prepare the eggplant. Place the eggs in a large bowl with a large pinch of salt and 2 tablespoons water and whisk well to combine. Place the bread crumbs in another bowl with a large pinch of salt and whisk well to combine. Working with one slice at a time, dip the eggplant in the egg and coat on both sides with the bread crumbs.

Pour 1 inch of olive oil into a large pot and heat the oil over medium-high heat. Test the oil: When a pinch of bread crumbs sizzles upon contact, it's ready. Add the breaded eggplant slices to the hot oil, working in batches as necessary to avoid crowding, and fry until dark golden brown and crisp, about 2 minutes per side. Transfer the eggplant slices to a paper towel–lined baking sheet to drain and sprinkle with salt.

To serve, place the eggplant slices on a serving platter. Divide the goat cheese among the pockets of the cooled peppers and place them on top of the crispy eggplant slices. Drizzle the peppers with their reserved cooking juices and sprinkle with the microgreens. Serve immediately.

Fried Baby Artichokes with Remoulade

Serves 4

Choose only the smallest, most tender young and green fresh artichokes. Once they have developed their purple choke inside, they're no longer as good.

¾ cup mayonnaise

1 celery stalk, minced

1 scallion, minced

2 tablespoons creole or Dijon mustard

1 tablespoon ketchup

A few dashes of hot sauce

2 tablespoons fresh lemon juice

Kosher salt and freshly ground black pepper

2 lemons, halved crosswise

1 pound baby artichokes

½ cup all-purpose flour

¼ cup cornstarch

½ cup olive oil

Place the mayonnaise, celery, scallion, mustard, ketchup, hot sauce, and lemon juice in a small bowl and whisk well to combine. Season with salt and pepper. Set aside.

Fill a large bowl with water and squeeze 2 of the lemon halves (1 whole lemon) into it (drop them straight into the bowl after you've squeezed out the juice).

Use a serrated knife to trim the top ¼ inch from each artichoke and trim off any remaining pointy tips. Tear off and discard the blemished outer leaves. Cut each artichoke in half through the stem and place them in the bowl of lemon water as you work (this will keep them from browning).

Place the flour, cornstarch, ½ teaspoon salt, ½ teaspoon pepper, and ½ cup water in a large bowl. Whisk well to combine.

Place the olive oil in a medium nonstick skillet and heat it over medium heat.

While the oil heats, working with one artichoke half at a time, lift the artichoke out of the lemon water and dip it into the batter to coat it (let the excess batter drip off). Transfer the battered artichokes to the hot oil, cut-side down, working in batches as necessary so you don't crowd the skillet. Cook until golden brown and crisp on the bottom, about 2 minutes, then carefully turn them over and cook until golden brown and crisp on the other side, about 2 minutes more. Transfer the fried artichokes to a paper towel–lined plated to drain and sprinkle them with a pinch of salt.

Transfer the artichokes to a serving platter. Place the remaining lemon halves on the platter for squeezing over and serve immediately with the remoulade alongside for dipping.

Tostones with Mojo Sauce

Serves 4

A Cuban version of chips and dip, these thick, crispy plantain chips (tostones) paired with super-garlicky mojo sauce are wonderful with a Frozen Paradise Paloma (page 311) at cocktail hour. The mojo sauce not only has a ton of garlic, it's also got fresh orange and lime juices and is excellent for marinating pork or beef or serving as a dipping sauce for either. It's also delicious drizzled on fried fish. The fried plantains themselves can be served without the mojo for an easy, fast side dish alongside any seafood or meat. Try just tossing them with some minced garlic, coarsely chopped cilantro, and a squeeze of fresh lime juice.

¼ cup fresh orange juice

¼ cup plus 2 tablespoons fresh lime juice

¼ cup olive oil

1 teaspoon kosher salt, plus more as needed

½ teaspoon minced fresh oregano, or ¼ teaspoon dried

¼ teaspoon ground cumin

12 garlic cloves, minced

2 tablespoons minced fresh cilantro

Neutral oil (such as canola or vegetable), for frying

1 green plantain, peeled and cut into 2-inch-thick rounds

½ cup crumbled queso blanco cheese, for serving

Place the orange juice, ¼ cup of the lime juice, the olive oil, salt, oregano, cumin, garlic, and 1 tablespoon of the cilantro in a medium bowl and whisk together. Set aside.

Pour 1 inch of neutral oil into a large heavy pot and heat the oil over medium-high heat. Test the oil: When a piece of plantain sizzles upon contact, it's ready. Add the plantain slices to the hot oil, working in batches as necessary to avoid crowding, and fry, turning the pieces now and then, until golden brown all over, about 3 minutes. Transfer the plantains to a paper towel and use the bottom of a small pot or a meat pounder to smash each plantain into a thin disc (be careful not to smash them too hard—you don't want them to break). Return the smashed plantains to the hot oil and fry, turning the pieces now and then, until crisp, about 3 minutes. Transfer the hot, crispy plantains to a large bowl and drizzle with the remaining 2 tablespoons lime juice. Sprinkle with a large pinch of salt and the remaining 1 tablespoon minced cilantro and toss well to combine.

Transfer the tostones to a serving platter, sprinkle with the queso blanco, and put the bowl of mojo next to them for dipping. Serve immediately.

Hollywood Burrata with Grated Tomato Dressing

Serves 4

Burrata is basically fresh mozzarella cheese that's formed into a pouch and filled with cream. Yep, you heard that right. As you can imagine, the best burrata is the freshest burrata, and it can be hard to track down (even the expensive stuff imported from Italy is, at minimum, a few days old, since it has to travel). When Carlo was writing the menu for JWB, he spent so much time tracking down the best ingredients and amazingly found that our local Italian product vendor makes their burrata every day. He placed a regular order, and now it's a fixture on the menu. The cheese is so good that it doesn't need much to make it shine. We adorn it simply with this amazingly easy grated tomato dressing. This is a perfect way to use overripe tomatoes since you're looking for flavor, not appearance. Also, if you can't track down fresh burrata, absolutely feel free to substitute fresh mozzarella cheese.

3 large vine-ripened tomatoes

½ teaspoon kosher salt, plus more if needed

1 small garlic clove, minced

3 tablespoons olive oil

Two 6-ounce balls fresh burrata cheese

Large handful of fresh basil leaves

½ pound thinly sliced prosciutto, for serving (optional)

Large pinch of freshly ground black pepper

Cut each tomato in half. Working over a large bowl, grate the cut side of each half on the coarse holes of a box grater. Discard the skins. Whisk the salt, garlic, and olive oil into the tomato pulp. Taste and season with more salt, if needed.

Place the tomato dressing on the bottom of the platter and top with the burrata, basil leaves, and prosciutto. Sprinkle everything with the black pepper and serve immediately.

Jalapeño Deviled Eggs with Pickled Mustard Seeds

Makes 24

Much more memorable than your typical deviled eggs, these have spicy, fresh jalapeño in and on them, plus pickled mustard seeds on top. The mustard seeds are much easier to make than they sound, and they not only add a briny, slightly spicy flavor to the eggs, but also some much-needed crunch. Plus, they help make something you see often look cooler than usual. You'll have some extra pickled mustard seeds left over from this recipe—use them to top a hot dog, grilled sausages, pastrami or corned beef sandwiches, or mix with mayonnaise and thin with some of the pickling liquid to make a delicious dipping sauce for crab claws or steamed shrimp.

FOR THE PICKLED MUSTARD SEEDS

¼ cup distilled white vinegar

1 tablespoon sugar

1 tablespoon kosher salt

½ cup yellow mustard seeds

FOR THE DEVILED EGGS

Kosher salt

12 large eggs

½ cup mayonnaise

1 teaspoon Worcestershire sauce

2 teaspoons fresh lemon juice

1 tablespoon Dijon mustard

1 tablespoon pickle relish

½ teaspoon garlic powder

A few grinds black pepper

1 jalapeño, seeded, ½ minced, ½ cut into thin slivers

MAKE THE PICKLED MUSTARD SEEDS: Place the vinegar, sugar, salt, and ¼ cup water in a small pot set over medium heat. Bring the mixture to a boil and then turn off the heat and stir in the mustard seeds. Let the mixture cool to room temperature. Use the mustard seeds immediately or transfer them to a container with the brine and refrigerate for up to 1 month. Drain the mustard seeds as you use them, just as you would capers.

(continued)

MAKE THE DEVILED EGGS: Bring a large pot of water to a boil and salt it generously. Fill a large bowl with ice and water. Add the eggs to the boiling water and cook for exactly 13 minutes, then use a slotted spoon to transfer them to the ice water. Let the eggs cool completely in the ice water, then drain and peel them. Cut each egg in half lengthwise and transfer the yolks to a large bowl. Set the whites aside on a serving platter, cut-side up.

Add the mayonnaise, Worcestershire, lemon juice, Dijon mustard, pickle relish, garlic powder, pepper, minced jalapeño, and $\frac{1}{2}$ teaspoon kosher salt to the bowl with the egg yolks. Whisk everything together until evenly blended. Transfer the mixture to a plastic bag and cut off the corner of the bag. Use the bag as if it were a pastry bag and pipe the filling into the egg white halves.

Top each deviled egg with a small spoonful of the pickled mustard seeds and a sliver of jalapeño. Serve immediately.

Cajun Chicken Quesadilla

We had Yucatán Quesadillas on our original Key West menu way back when. They featured braised and pulled chicken (much like the Chicken Tinga on page 189). While they were delicious, they required a lot of work to prepare. These are inspired by them, with a detour to Louisiana, and require a whole lot less preparation (which makes them much more appealing for us home cooks). If you'd like, though, you can absolutely substitute Chicken Tinga for the Cajun-spiced chicken. The double baking sheet method is explained in the Spicy Breakfast Quesadillas (page 24), but feel free to just sear these in a skillet on the stovetop if you prefer (the double baking sheets let you cook them all at once).

2 boneless, skinless chicken breasts

4 teaspoons Blackening Seasoning (recipe follows)

1 tablespoon neutral oil (such as canola or vegetable), for frying

Cooking spray

Eight 6-inch flour tortillas

1 cup coarsely grated Monterey Jack cheese

1 cup coarsely grated sharp cheddar cheese

1 cup drained Fajita Black Beans (page 255) or drained and rinsed canned black beans, warmed

½ small red onion, thinly sliced

Sour cream, for serving

Guacamole (page 241), for serving

Pico de Gallo (page 238), for serving

Preheat the oven to 400°F. Place two baking sheets in the oven to heat up.

Evenly sprinkle the chicken breasts with the blackening seasoning. Place the oil in a medium cast-iron skillet set over medium-high heat. Once it's nice and hot, add the chicken breasts. Cook, turning them once, until blackened on both sides and firm to the touch, about 4 minutes per side. Transfer the chicken to a plate and let it rest for at least 10 minutes while you get everything else set up.

Take one of the hot baking sheets out of the oven and spray it with cooking spray. Place 4 of the tortillas on the hot baking sheet in a single layer (it's okay if they overlap slightly) and evenly sprinkle half of both of the cheeses over the surface of each tortilla. Evenly divide the black beans and onions among the tortillas, being sure to put them on only half of each tortilla. Thinly slice the chicken breasts and divide the chicken among the tortillas. Evenly divide the remaining cheese between the quesadillas. Top each quesadilla with another tortilla. Spray the top of each quesadilla with cooking spray and stack the other hot baking sheet on top on them so that the quesadillas make contact on both sides with the hot baking sheet.

Place the quesadillas, sandwiched between the baking sheets, into the oven and bake until both sides are golden brown and the cheese is melted, about 10 minutes.

Cut each quesadilla into wedges and serve immediately with sour cream, guacamole, and pico de gallo alongside.

Blackening Seasoning

Essential not only for our Cajun Chicken Quesadilla (page 91), this seasoning mixture is also key for the fish in the Blackened Fish Sandwiches (page 152) and of course our Blackened Chili Dogs (page 159). Try it anytime you grill or panfry chicken, pork, or fish. In fact, feel free to double or even quadruple the batch so you have extra to sprinkle any- and everywhere.

1 teaspoon paprika

1 teaspoon kosher salt

½ teaspoon cayenne pepper

½ teaspoon garlic powder

½ teaspoon freshly ground black pepper

½ teaspoon dried thyme

Place everything in a small bowl and stir together. Store in a covered jar at room temperature for up to 2 months.

Spicy Buffalo Chicken Wings
with Buttermilk Blue Cheese Dressing

Serves 4

You know what they say about fixing things that aren't broken. . . . These are straightforward, old-fashioned chicken wings. Our big trick is heating the hot sauce and blending it with cold butter to make an emulsified mixture that's wonderfully thick and coats the wings beautifully. If you don't want to dirty the blender, though, you can just melt the butter with the hot sauce and whisk the two together. They'll still be great.

5 tablespoons unsalted butter, cut into cubes

½ cup hot sauce (preferably Frank's RedHot or Crystal)

1 teaspoon cayenne pepper

Neutral oil (such as canola or vegetable), for frying

2 pounds chicken wings, wing tips discarded, halved at the joint, patted dry with paper towels

Celery sticks, for serving

Buttermilk Blue Cheese Dressing (recipe follows), for serving

Place the butter in a blender. Place the hot sauce and cayenne in a small pot set over high heat. When it comes to a boil, turn off the heat and add it to the blender. Blend until smooth. (Alternatively, you can place the butter in the pot and use a handheld blender to combine everything.) Set aside.

Pour 1 inch of oil into a large heavy pot and heat the oil over medium heat. Test the oil: When a chicken wing sizzles upon contact, it's ready. Add as many wings as will fit in an even, not-crowded layer. Fry the wings, turning them a few times while they cook, until golden brown all over, about 12 minutes. Regulate the heat while they're frying so that the oil is hot enough to bubble around the edges of the chicken, but not so hot that the chicken burns. Transfer the wings to a paper towel–lined plate to drain. Break into one to make sure it's cooked through (if it's not, throw the batch back into the oil and continue to cook until they're done). Repeat the process, adding more oil to the pot as needed, until you've fried all your wings.

Put the fried wings in a large bowl and drizzle with the butter–hot sauce mixture. Toss well to combine. Transfer to a serving platter and serve immediately, with celery sticks and Buttermilk Blue Cheese Dressing alongside. And lots of napkins.

Buttermilk Blue Cheese Dressing

Makes about 2 cups

Simple and classic, this is perfect blue cheese dressing. It's not only required with spicy chicken wings, it's also an essential component of our Little Gem Wedge Salad (page 107) and our Black-and-Blue Burgers (page 131). It can also be used as a dip for crudité or as a dressing on a platter of sliced tomatoes. Serve topped with extra chives.

½ cup buttermilk

½ cup mayonnaise

¼ cup sour cream

1 teaspoon granulated garlic

½ teaspoon kosher salt

½ teaspoon freshly ground black pepper

2 teaspoons white balsamic vinegar (or white wine vinegar)

¾ cup crumbled blue cheese

1 tablespoon minced fresh chives

Place the buttermilk, mayonnaise, sour cream, granulated garlic, salt, pepper, and vinegar in a large bowl and whisk well to combine. Stir in the blue cheese and chives. Serve immediately or store in an airtight container in the fridge for up to 1 week.

Sweet Chile Chicken Wings

A Southeast Asian spin on chicken wings, this version swaps the typical hot sauce-and-butter mixture for a combination of sweet chile sauce and spicy chile paste. A platter of cool, crunchy cucumber slices would be a nice accompaniment in the same way celery stalks usually complement hot wings. For a complete meal, serve these with a pot of rice and a bowl of Cilantro-Lime Coleslaw (page 242).

½ cup sweet chile sauce (preferably Mae Ploy brand)

1 tablespoon chile paste (preferably sambal oelek)

2 pounds chicken wings, wing tips discarded, halved at the joint, patted dry with paper towels

Neutral oil (such as canola or vegetable), for frying

1 lime, cut into wedges, for serving

Place the chile sauce and chile paste in a large bowl . Whisk to combine and set aside.

Pour 1 inch of oil into a large heavy pot and heat the oil over medium heat. Test the oil: When a chicken wing sizzles upon contact, it's ready. Add as many wings as can fit in an even, not-crowded layer. Fry the wings, turning them a few times while they cook, until golden brown all over, about 12 minutes. Regulate the heat while they're frying so that the oil is hot enough to bubble around the edges of the chicken, but not so hot that the chicken burns. Transfer the wings to a paper towel–lined plate to drain. Break into one to make sure it's cooked through (if it's not, throw the batch back into the oil and continue to cook until they're done). Repeat the process, adding more oil to the pot as needed, until you've fried all your wings.

Put the wings in the bowl with the chile sauce mixture. Toss well to combine.

Transfer to a serving platter. Serve immediately, with lime wedges for squeezing over and plenty of napkins.

Salads & Soups

"BAROMETER'S MY SOUP. . . ."

Sometimes there's nothing better than a big chopped salad on a hot day eaten on a deck with an iced tea, just like the good way it feels to have a warm bowl of soup in front of a fireplace when it's chilly outside. We love tapping into this sense of comfort and also adding whatever little unexpected twists we can find to make the usual a little bit more special. Take the JWB House Salad (page 105) served at the Margaritaville Hollywood Beach Resort. Instead of plain old salad dressing, Carlo devised a creamy mixture of salted cashews, miso paste, and tahini paste that's rich, addictive, and a little hard to put your finger on. Or our Bahamian Conch Chowder (page 119), which puts conch front and center along with fresh tomatoes and coconut milk. There are plenty of tried-and-true classics in this chapter, too, including Carlo's Caesar salad (page 102), and tons of new favorites like the Avocado and Papaya Salad with Spicy Lime Dressing (page 108), which is as easy to make as it is a joy to eat.

JWB Caesar Salad with Sourdough Croutons

Serves 4

Classic Caesar salad is all about the marriage of rich dressing, crunchy croutons, and crisp lettuce, and this one is an example of Carlo's embrace of not messing with perfection. Like the Lemon Aioli (page 58), this includes a raw egg yolk. Make sure it's pasteurized (which the US Department of Agriculture considers safe to consume). If raw egg presents a health issue for you, simply whisk the garlic, mustard, anchovies, vinegar, scallion, and Worcestershire sauce into a cup of prepared mayonnaise.

FOR THE CROUTONS

4 cups bite-size cubes sourdough bread

¼ cup finely grated Parmesan cheese

¼ cup olive oil

FOR THE DRESSING

1 large egg yolk

1 small garlic clove, minced

½ teaspoon Dijon mustard

2 oil-packed anchovy fillets, drained and mashed with a fork

2 teaspoons white wine vinegar

1 scallion, finely chopped

2 teaspoons Worcestershire sauce

¼ cup olive oil

½ cup neutral oil (such as canola or vegetable)

Kosher salt

FOR THE SALAD

2 large hearts of romaine lettuce, leaves separated

½ cup shaved Parmesan cheese

MAKE THE CROUTONS: Preheat the oven to 350°F. Place the bread and Parmesan on a parchment-lined baking sheet and drizzle with the olive oil. Use your hands to toss everything together. Bake the croutons, stirring now and then, until golden brown, 10 to 15 minutes. Let the croutons cool to room temperature on the pan (they will crisp as they cool).

MAKE THE DRESSING: Place the egg yolk, garlic, mustard, anchovies, vinegar, scallion, and Worcestershire in a large bowl and whisk until everything is thoroughly combined. While whisking, slowly drizzle in the oils to form a smooth, emulsified dressing. Season the dressing with salt.

MAKE THE SALAD: Place the croutons and the romaine in the large bowl with the dressing. Toss gently to combine and divide among four serving plates and top each with shaved Parmesan cheese.

JWB House Salad with Cashew Dressing

It's surprising to find a salad dressing this rich and creamy that also happens to be completely vegan. It is a testament to the power of the cashew! When blended with a little water, cashews become smoother than you can even imagine. Combined with acidic rice vinegar, assertive miso paste, and nutty tahini paste, the dressing is a lesson in flavor.

½ cup salted cashews plus 3 tablespoons, coarsely chopped

Pinch of sugar

2 teaspoons finely grated lemon zest

1½ tablespoons malt vinegar

1½ tablespoons seasoned rice vinegar

1 tablespoon white miso paste

1 tablespoon tahini paste

1 tablespoon walnut oil

Kosher salt

1 bunch asparagus, tough ends discarded, cut into 1-inch pieces

5 ounces mixed greens

1 small red onion, thinly sliced

1 large carrot, thinly sliced

Place the ½ cup of cashews in a high-speed blender with ½ cup water and blend until smooth. Add the sugar, lemon zest and vinegars and blend until well incorporated. Add the miso, tahini, and walnut oil and blend until smooth. Season the dressing with salt and pour it into a large bowl.

Meanwhile, bring a large pot of water to a boil and add a few large pinches of salt. Add the asparagus and cook until bright green and tender, about 1 minute. Drain the asparagus in a colander and rinse with cold water to stop the cooking. Dry on a kitchen towel.

Add the blanched asparagus along with the greens, onion, and carrots to the bowl of dressing. Gently mix everything together and serve immediately topped with the remaining chopped cashews.

Little Gem Wedge Salad

Wedge salad usual involves big pieces of iceberg, but we love using adorable heads of Little Gem lettuce instead since they have all the same crunch with a little bit more flavor. If you can't track down Little Gem, quartered hearts of romaine work. Also, we like the yolks in our eggs a little bit soft, so we cook them for just 6 minutes. If you prefer them more cooked, simply leave the eggs in the water for an extra 5 minutes.

4 large eggs

12 heads Little Gem lettuce, quartered lengthwise, or 3 hearts of romaine, quartered lengthwise

1 cup Buttermilk Blue Cheese Dressing (page 96)

1 cup grape tomatoes, halved

¼ cup crumbled Danish blue cheese

Small handful of fresh chives, finely chopped

Fill a large bowl with ice and water. Place the eggs in a small saucepan and add cold water to cover. Bring the water to a boil over high heat. Cover the pot, turn off the heat, and let the eggs sit for exactly 6 minutes. Use a slotted spoon to transfer the eggs to the ice water and let cool until they're easy to handle. Peel the eggs and coarsely chop them.

Arrange the lettuce, cut-sides up, on a serving platter (or on four individual salad plates) and drizzle half the dressing over them. Top with the grape tomatoes, blue cheese, and chopped eggs. Drizzle with the remaining dressing, sprinkle with the chives, and serve immediately.

Avocado and Papaya Salad with Spicy Lime Dressing

A beautiful salad, this is all about the rich texture of ripe avocados and papayas balanced with a tart, spicy dressing. Since it's so simple, it relies on perfectly ripe fruit. Look for heavy avocados that yield to very gentle pressure. The same goes for your papaya, and also look out for skin that's yellow-orange with a few brown spots. Serve this with grilled fish, shrimp, or chicken for a nice light lunch.

3 tablespoons fresh lime juice

1½ tablespoons chile paste (preferably Sambal Oelek)

2 teaspoons honey

¼ cup plus 2 tablespoons olive oil

1 teaspoon kosher salt

1 shallot, minced

1 large ripe papaya, peeled, seeded, and diced

2 ripe avocados, pitted, peeled, and diced

Small handful of fresh mint leaves

Small handful of fresh cilantro leaves

Freshly ground black pepper

Place the lime juice, chile paste, honey, olive oil, and ½ teaspoon of the salt in a small bowl and whisk together. Stir in the shallot and set the dressing aside.

Arrange the papaya and avocado on a serving platter and evenly sprinkle with the remaining ½ teaspoon salt. Drizzle evenly with the dressing and then sprinkle with the herbs. Top with a few grinds of black pepper. Serve immediately.

Quinoa and Mango Salad with Seared Tuna

Feel free to swap grilled chicken or steak for the tuna in this colorful chopped salad. Or keep things vegetarian—between the quinoa, garbanzo beans, and cheese, this salad is plenty substantial and satisfying on its own. Look for queso fresco in the cheese section of your grocery store, near other Mexican cheeses like cotija.

2 large handfuls of fresh cilantro leaves

2 tablespoons fresh lemon juice

2 teaspoons honey

2 teaspoons Dijon mustard

1 teaspoon ground cumin

Kosher salt and freshly ground black pepper

¼ cup olive oil

1 cup coarsely chopped sugar snap peas

1 cup cooked quinoa

5 ounces baby kale

1 cup canned, drained and rinsed garbanzo beans

½ large cucumber, seeded and diced

½ small red onion, finely diced

1 small red bell pepper, finely diced

¾ cup crumbled queso fresco

1 mango, pitted, peeled, and diced

Four 4-ounce fresh sushi-grade ahi tuna steaks

2 tablespoons neutral oil (such as canola or vegetable), for frying

Place 1 handful of the cilantro, the lemon juice, honey, mustard, cumin, 2 tablespoons water, ½ teaspoon kosher salt, and a few grinds of black pepper in a medium bowl. Whisk well to combine. While whisking, slowly drizzle in the olive oil to make a smooth dressing. (Alternatively, you can combine all the ingredients in a blender and blend together.)

Bring a small pot of water to a boil. Add the peas and cook just until bright green, about 30 seconds. Drain the snap peas and rinse them under cool running water to stop the cooking. Transfer to a paper towel to dry and then place them in a large salad bowl. Add the quinoa, kale, beans, cucumber, red onion, bell pepper, queso fresco, mango, and remaining cilantro. Drizzle with three-quarters of the dressing and stir gently to combine.

Season the tuna steaks aggressively on both sides with salt and black pepper. Place the neutral oil in a large heavy skillet set over high heat. Working in batches if necessary, depending on the size of your skillet, sear the tuna steaks until browned on both sides, about 1 minute per side. They should still be rare inside. Transfer the tuna steaks to a cutting board and cut them into 1-inch cubes. Add the tuna to the salad and stir gently to combine.

Divide the salad among four shallow bowls or plates. Drizzle the remaining dressing over them. Serve immediately.

Fried Green Tomato Salad with Salsa Verde and Queso Fresco

Serves 4

In this green-meets-green salad, crispy fried green tomatoes get topped with our tomatillo-based Salsa Verde. If you can't track down queso fresco, crumbled feta cheese makes an excellent substitute. Serve this along with a pot of Chicken and Corn Chupe (page 121) for a salad-and-soup meal.

1 cup stone-ground cornmeal

1 cup all-purpose flour

1 tablespoon garlic powder

¼ teaspoon cayenne pepper

1½ cups buttermilk

1 teaspoon kosher salt

½ teaspoon freshly ground black pepper

4 large green tomatoes, cored and cut into ¼-inch-thick slices

½ cup neutral oil (such as canola or vegetable), plus more if needed, for frying

1 large head radicchio, thinly sliced

1 large head frisée, coarsely chopped

2 tablespoons fresh lime juice

Small handful of fresh cilantro leaves

1 cup crumbled queso fresco

1½ cups Salsa Verde (page 187)

Place the cornmeal, flour, garlic powder, and cayenne in a baking dish and whisk together.

Place the buttermilk, salt, and pepper in a medium bowl and whisk together.

Working with one green tomato slice at a time, dip the green tomatoes in the buttermilk mixture and then dredge both sides in the cornmeal mixture.

Place the oil in a large nonstick skillet set over medium-high heat. Test the oil: When the edge of a breaded tomato sizzles upon contact, it's ready. Add the breaded tomato slices to the hot oil, working in batches as necessary to prevent crowding, and fry until dark golden brown and crisp, about 2 minutes per side. Transfer the tomato slices to a paper towel–lined baking sheet to drain. Fry the rest of the tomatoes, adding more oil to the skillet if necessary between batches.

Place the radicchio and frisée on a large serving platter and drizzle with the lime juice. Mix the salad well with your hands and then place the fried green tomatoes on top. Top with the cilantro and queso fresco. Serve immediately with the salsa verde for drizzling on top.

Andalusian Gazpacho

Refrigerating the ingredients all together before blending helps chill them down so you can enjoy the gazpacho immediately; plus, it helps all the flavors combine. You can, however, blend everything and then refrigerate until very cold before serving. Serve on a hot day! If you'd like to add a bit more heft to this, you can add some cooked crabmeat or shrimp to each serving. See the note after the recipe for a cucumber version.

1 pound fresh tomatoes, cored, coarsely chopped

1 small red onion, finely diced

2 garlic cloves, minced

1 medium cucumber, peeled, half coarsely chopped and half finely diced for serving

2 small red bell peppers, 1 coarsely chopped and 1 finely diced for serving

2 jarred piquillo peppers, drained and coarsely chopped

¼ cup sherry vinegar

2 tablespoons olive oil, plus more for serving

1 teaspoon sugar

1½ teaspoons kosher salt

1 teaspoon freshly ground black pepper

1 avocado, pitted, peeled, and coarsely chopped

1 cup small croutons

Small handful of microgreens (or coarsely chopped fresh parsley)

Place the tomatoes, onion, garlic, coarsely chopped cucumber, chopped red bell pepper, piquillo peppers, sherry vinegar, olive oil, sugar, salt, and black pepper in a blender container and add 1½ cups cold water. Cover and refrigerate for at least 4 hours or up to 12 hours.

Puree the cold mixture until very smooth. Taste and season the gazpacho with more salt and/or vinegar as needed. Divide the gazpacho among four bowls. Divide the avocado, croutons, microgreens, finely diced cucumber, and finely diced red bell pepper among the bowls. Drizzle each serving with about 2 teaspoons olive oil. Serve immediately.

Variation: For a chilled cucumber soup, gazpacho's twin, place a peeled, seeded, and coarsely chopped cucumber in a blender with a handful of mint leaves, a peeled, cored, and chopped green apple, and a small handful of minced red onion. Add about 1 cup plain yogurt and a healthy splash of sherry vinegar and puree until smooth. If the mixture is too thick, add some water to thin it out. Season with kosher salt and freshly ground black pepper and refrigerate until cold.

Luxurious Lobster Bisque

Serves 4

Making this bisque is a lesson in old-school cooking. The homemade stock gets mixed with sherry, cognac, and cream. Layer upon layer of flavor, this bisque is what to make for someone you want to impress or just show how much you care about them. This stock is useful for more than just this bisque. If you're going to do the work to make it, make extra and freeze it! Use it as a pasta sauce (add the lobster meat and a little broccoli rabe and top with crunchy bread crumbs). Or use the stock for a delicious seafood stew. Sauté whatever is fresh and good in a little garlic and oil and then drown it in the stock. Delicious. The xanthan gum works as a wonderful stabilizer and keeps the bisque very smooth and creamy (it's widely available at stores like Whole Foods and Trader Joe's). If you can't find it, though, just substitute 2 teaspoons cornstarch mixed with 2 tablespoons cold water.

8 cups Lobster Stock (recipe follows)

2 tablespoons dry or cream sherry

3 tablespoons cognac

1½ teaspoons minced fresh tarragon

¼ cup heavy cream

2 tablespoons unsalted butter

¼ teaspoon xanthan gum

Kosher salt and freshly ground black pepper

Coarse sugar (preferably turbinado) or granulated sugar

½ pound cooked lobster tail meat, coarsely chopped

4 tablespoons crème fraîche (or sour cream)

2 tablespoons minced fresh chives

Place the stock, sherry, and cognac in a large pot set over high heat and bring to a boil. Boil for 4 minutes to cook off the alcohol and then reduce the heat to maintain a simmer. Stir in the tarragon, cream, butter, and xanthan gum. Taste and season the soup with salt, pepper, and sugar. Divide the soup, cooked lobster, crème fraîche, and chives between 4 bowls. Serve immediately.

Lobster Stock

Makes about 8 cups

Any time you cook or eat a lobster, save the heads for this stock. It is not only the base for Luxurious Lobster Bisque (page 116), it also makes such a difference in the Paella del Mar (page 222) or anywhere else you would use lobster or seafood stock. It's nice to get a little extra life out of such an expensive ingredient, especially from the part you don't normally eat.

4 lobster heads (preferably from Maine lobsters)

2 tablespoons olive oil

1 teaspoon coarse sugar (preferably turbinado) or granulated sugar

2 teaspoons kosher salt

2 celery stalks, finely diced

2 carrots, finely diced

1 large yellow onion, finely diced

4 garlic cloves, minced

2 tablespoons tomato paste

1 teaspoon freshly ground black pepper

¼ cup brandy

½ cup white wine (preferably Chardonnay)

Small handful of fresh parsley, coarsely chopped

Cut the lobster heads in half and remove and discard soft brown matter and the gills. Rinse the heads under cold running water and set them aside.

Place the olive oil in a large pot set over medium-high heat. Once it's hot, add the cleaned lobster heads and sprinkle with the sugar. Cook, stirring, until the shells are bright red and smell incredibly fragrant, about 8 minutes. Add the salt, celery, carrot, onion, garlic, tomato paste, and pepper. Cook, stirring, until the vegetables begin to soften, about 5 minutes. Add the brandy and cook until it has nearly evaporated, about 4 minutes. Add the wine, parsley, and 10 cups cold water and bring to a boil, scraping the bottom of the pot with a wooden spoon to dislodge anything that's stuck. Reduce the heat to maintain a simmer and cook the stock until it has reduced by one-quarter, 2½ to 3 hours. Remove and discard the lobster heads and then transfer the rest of the mixture to a blender (work in batches if necessary) and puree until smooth. Strain the stock through a fine-mesh sieve. Use immediately or let cool to room temperature, then transfer to airtight containers and refrigerate for up to 3 days or freeze for up to 1 month.

Bahamian Conch Chowder

Serves 6 to 8

The best of all worlds, this chowder has all the wonderful tomato-forward characteristices of Manhattan clam chowder, plus the island flavor and creamy appeal of New England–style chowder thanks to a can of coconut milk. With plenty of conch instead of clams and lots of fresh vegetables for texture and color, a bowl of this chowder is the easiest way to escape to the Bahamas. If you have extra conch, make a batch of Conch Fritters with Calypso Sauce (page 48).

4 tablespoons (½ stick) unsalted butter

3 cups conch (drained if canned or thawed and drained if frozen), finely chopped

1 large carrot, finely diced

1 small red onion, finely diced

1 small green bell pepper, finely diced

2 garlic cloves, minced

3 medium Yukon Gold potatoes, peeled and cut into ½-inch dice

4 cups diced fresh tomatoes, or one 28-ounce can diced tomatoes in juice

1 teaspoon dried oregano

1 teaspoon dried thyme

1 teaspoon kosher salt, plus more if needed

½ teaspoon cayenne pepper

Four 8-ounce bottles clam juice (4 cups)

One 13½-ounce can full-fat coconut milk

2 cups tomato juice

Place the butter in a large soup pot set over medium heat. Once it melts, add the conch, carrot, onion, bell pepper, and garlic. Cook, stirring now and then, until the vegetables are softened, about 10 minutes. Add the potatoes, diced tomatoes, oregano, thyme, salt, cayenne, clam juice, coconut milk, and tomato juice. Stir well to combine. Raise the heat to high and bring the mixture to a boil. Once it boils, reduce the heat to low and simmer until the potatoes are just tender, about 15 minutes. Season the with salt and serve hot.

Chicken and Corn Chupe

Serves 6 to 8

Chupe (choo-pay), a Peruvian chowder is very comforting and is what Carlo suggests having after a long night out. There are three forms of corn in this: fresh corn on the cob, canned sweet corn, and corn chips. The sum of their parts is a study in corn. Put a bottle of Tabasco (or your favorite hot sauce) on the table when you serve this soup, as a little heat really balances the sweetness of the corn beautifully. You can also make this with clams instead of chicken for a clam-and-corn chowder.

7 cups high-quality store-bought chicken stock

2 ½ pounds chicken thighs and drumsticks

3 tablespoons olive oil

4 garlic cloves, minced

1 large red onion, thinly sliced

2 tablespoons unsalted butter

½ cup coarsely chopped fresh cilantro

Kosher salt

1 tablespoon freshly ground black pepper

3 ears fresh corn, shucked, cut into 1-inch discs

Two 16-ounce cans sweet corn

2 cups whole milk

5 ounces corn tortilla chips (about 3 cups)

¼ cup fresh lemon juice

Place the stock and chicken in a large pot set over high heat and bring to a boil. Reduce the heat to maintain a simmer and cook until the chicken is just cooked through, about 25 minutes. Use tongs to transfer the chicken to a bowl and set aside to cool. Keep the stock warm over low heat. When the chicken is cool enough to handle, remove and discard the skin and bones; shred or coarsely chop the meat and set it aside.

Meanwhile, place the olive oil and garlic in a large pot set over medium heat. Once the garlic sizzles, add the red onion and butter. Cook, stirring now and then, until the onion is translucent, about 10 minutes. Add 3 tablespoons of the chopped cilantro, 1 tablespoon salt, the pepper, and the fresh corn. Cook, stirring now and then, until the corn is bright yellow and the kernels are tender, about 10 minutes.

Drain the cans of corn, reserving 1 cup of the canning liquid. Place the drained corn and the reserved liquid into the pot with the onions and fresh corn. Add the milk, the reserved chicken, and the warm stock and increase the heat to high. Bring the mixture to a boil, then reduce the heat to maintain a simmer and cook for 35 minutes to let all of the flavors combine and develop.

Add half of the corn chips and lemon juice to the pot and stir to combine and soften the chips. Use an immersion blender to puree some of the soup to thicken it and give the consistency of chowder (or ladle about 2 cups of the soup into a standard blender, puree it, and then return it to the pot). Avoid the fresh corn when blending. Season the soup with salt. Ladle it into bowls and top each one with some of the remaining corn chips and remaining chopped cilantro.

Burgers,
Sandwiches &
Hot Dogs

"NOT TOO PARTICULAR, NOT TOO PRECISE, I'M JUST A CHEESEBURGER IN PARADISE...."

At our core, we're all about casual food and good times. Which means we care a lot about things like great burgers and memorable sandwiches, since they're easy and fun to eat and are usually what everyone is craving. Sometimes a sandwich can take you right back to a particular moment in time. In fact, some of the best stories from Margaritaville's history are in this chapter. There's the time Jimmy got stranded in Tortola and ended up having a Cheeseburger in Paradise (page 126), and plenty of New Orleans lore comes along with the Tailgate Muffuletta for a Crowd (page 145) and the New Orleans Fried Oyster Po'Boys (page 149). And since we believe in the power of combining the best things, there are some really inventive sandwiches in this chapter, including the Delta Fried Catfish Reubens (page 150). There are also high-end sandwiches like our JWB Lobster Rolls (page 155). Rounded out with some of our favorite hot dogs from our Floridays hot dog stand in Hollywood Beach, Florida, this chapter includes all the best things since sliced bread (and buns).

Cheeseburgers in Paradise
with Paradise Island Dressing

Serves 4

The Cheeseburger in Paradise story has been passed down, and it changes a bit in each telling. Here is the real story, straight from Jimmy:

Back in 1974, I sailed into Roadtown, Tortola, after a few days of hard weather. We were tired and hungry, but in those days, gourmet restaurants were few and far between in the British Virgin Islands. So it was with a great deal of excitement when we read in the cruising guide of the new Village Cay marina and restaurant in Roadtown. We tied up our boat and dashed for the patio, where we feasted on burgers and the available accoutrements. Regardless of what other stories you have heard, that is the story of the real birth of the cheeseburger in paradise that was put to song. I know. I was there.

Each and every time we make a cheeseburger, we want it to taste as good as the one Jimmy had. We make sure this happens by using really high-quality ground beef and seasoning it liberally with our House Spice Blend (which would make anything taste good), and then we're generous with cheese and our Paradise Island Dressing. Don't forget to have lots of napkins handy.

1½ pounds ground beef

1 tablespoon Margaritaville House Spice Blend (page 128)

2 tablespoons neutral oil (such as canola or vegetable), for frying

8 slices cheese (we like American)

½ cup Paradise Island Dressing (page 129)

4 burger buns, split and lightly toasted

2 cups shredded iceberg lettuce

8 large tomato slices

Dill pickle slices, for serving

Divide the ground beef into 4 even portions and shape each into a patty. Sprinkle both sides of each burger with some of the spice blend.

Place the oil in a large cast-iron skillet that can hold the burgers in a single layer (or work in batches or use two skillets). Set the skillet over high heat and turn your exhaust fan on. Once the skillet is smoking hot, place the burgers in the skillet and cook until the undersides are nicely browned, 2 to 3 minutes. Carefully turn the burgers and top each one with 2 slices of cheese. Cook until the second sides are nicely browned and the cheese has melted, 2 to 4 minutes more.

Divide the Paradise Island Dressing between the cut sides of the buns and spread to cover. Put ½ cup of the shredded lettuce on the bottom half of each bun and top with a cheeseburger. Top each cheeseburger with a couple slices of tomato. Top with the top buns and then close the burgers. Serve immediately with pickle slices alongside.

Margaritaville House Spice Blend

Welcome to the spice blend that makes our burgers taste as good as they do, not to mention everything else it goes on. Try using it anywhere you would normally just use salt and pepper. It will help even the simplest things like grilled chicken shine. Store the spice blend in a closed container at room temperature in a dark spot for up to 2 months. Feel free to double or even quadruple the batch!

2 tablespoons onion powder

2 tablespoons garlic powder

1 tablespoon kosher salt

1 tablespoon ground cumin

Place all the ingredients in a bowl and whisk together.

Paradise Island Dressing

Our take on Thousand Island dressing, this version gets a healthy dose of lime juice to make it just a bit more fresh-tasting and give it a slightly tropical vibe.

½ cup mayonnaise

¼ cup ketchup

2 tablespoons pickle relish

2 tablespoons fresh lime juice, plus more if needed

½ teaspoon kosher salt, plus more if needed

Place all the ingredients together in a large bowl and whisk together. Taste for seasoning and add more lime and/or salt as needed.

Black-and-Blue Burgers

Not your ordinary bacon cheeseburger, these black-and-blue burgers combine spicy black pepper bacon with blue cheese *and* Buttermilk Blue Cheese Dressing. If you're afraid of flavor, this is not the burger for you. . . .

8 slices black pepper bacon

1½ pounds ground beef

1 tablespoon Margaritaville House Spice Blend (page 128)

4 burger buns, split and lightly toasted

¼ cup Buttermilk Blue Cheese Dressing (page 96), plus extra for serving

4 large Bibb or green-leaf lettuce leaves

8 large tomato slices

½ cup crumbled Danish blue cheese

Place the bacon in a large cast-iron skillet set over medium-high heat. Cook, turning the bacon a few times while it cooks, until crisp, about 5 minutes. Use tongs to transfer the bacon to a paper towel–lined plate. Leave the fat in the skillet and set aside.

Divide the ground beef into 4 even portions and shape each into a patty. Sprinkle both sides of each burger with some of the spice blend.

Set the skillet back over high heat and turn your exhaust fan on. Once it's smoking hot, place the burgers in the skillet and cook until the bottoms are nicely browned, 2 to 3 minutes. Carefully turn the burgers and cook until the second side is nicely browned, 2 to 4 minutes more.

Spread 1 tablespoon of the Buttermilk Blue Cheese Dressing on the bottom half of each burger bun and top with a lettuce leaf and a burger. Top each burger with 2 slices of tomato, 2 table-spoons of crumbled blue cheese, and 2 slices of bacon. Close the burgers and serve immediately with extra dressing alongside.

Turkey Burgers with Cheddar and Barbecue Aioli

Serves 4

Most turkey burgers tend to be kind of boring, quite flavorless, and dry. Not this one! We put plenty of Margaritaville House Spice Blend (page 128) both into and on top of the burgers and top them extra-sharp cheese and lots of barbecue aioli. The result is a juicy, can't-put-it-down burger that will satisfy even the most red meat-loving eaters.

¼ cup barbecue sauce (preferably Margaritaville brand Original Flavor)

¼ cup mayonnaise

1 teaspoon cayenne pepper

1½ pounds ground turkey (preferably dark meat)

2 tablespoons Margaritaville House Spice Blend (page 128)

2 tablespoons neutral oil (such as canola or vegetable)

4 burger buns, split and lightly toasted

4 slices extra-sharp cheddar cheese

4 large Bibb or green-leaf lettuce leaves

8 large tomato slices

8 very thin slices raw red onion

Place the barbecue sauce, mayonnaise, and cayenne in a small bowl and whisk together. Set aside.

Place the ground turkey into a large bowl, sprinkle with 1 tablespoon of the spice blend, and mix well to combine. Divide the turkey into 4 even portions and shape each into a patty. Sprinkle both sides of each burger with some of the remaining spice blend.

Place the oil in a large cast-iron skillet that can hold the burgers in a single layer (or work in batches or use two skillets). Set the skillet over medium-high heat and turn your exhaust fan on. Once the skillet is hot, place the burgers in the skillet and cook until the bottoms are nicely browned, about 4 minutes. Carefully turn the burgers and cook until the second side is nicely browned and the burgers are firm to the touch, 4 minutes more. Top each burger with a slice of cheddar, reduce the heat to low, cover the skillet, and cook until the cheese has melted, 1 minute more.

Divide the barbecue aioli among the buns and spread to cover both cut sides of each. Put a slice of lettuce on the bottom half of each burger bun and top with a turkey burger. Top each one with 2 slices each onion and tomato. Close the burgers and serve immediately.

JWB Surf 'n' Turf Burgers

If you're looking for a high-end burger, we've got you. Our handheld version of classic surf 'n' turf, this is our steakhouse's answer to a classic burger. Serve with Oven Fries (page 254).

1½ pounds ground beef

1½ tablespoons JWB Steak Seasoning (page 171), or 1½ teaspoons kosher salt plus 1 teaspoon freshly ground black pepper

4 large asparagus spears, tough ends discarded, halved crosswise

1 tablespoon olive oil

1 tablespoon fresh lemon juice

3 tablespoons unsalted butter

2 shelled Maine lobster tails, halved lengthwise

½ teaspoon kosher salt

4 onions rolls, split

½ cup Key Lime Hollandaise (page 20), warmed

4 Bibb lettuce leaves

Preheat an outdoor grill to high or set a grill pan over high heat.

Divide the ground beef into 4 even portions and shape each into a patty. Using 1 tablespoon of the steak seasoning, season both sides of the burgers.

Place the asparagus in a large bowl and drizzle with the olive oil and lemon juice. Sprinkle with the remaining ½ tablespoon steak seasoning. Toss well to combine.

Grill the burgers until just firm to the touch and nicely browned on both sides, about 3 minutes per side. Grill the asparagus until just softened and browned all over, about 1 minute per side. Transfer the burgers and asparagus to a wire rack set over a baking sheet and keep them nearby.

While you're grilling the burgers, place the butter in a large nonstick skillet set over medium heat. Once it melts, add the lobster tail pieces and sprinkle with the salt. Cook, turning the pieces now and then, until just firm to the touch and opaque, about 4 minutes. Transfer the lobster pieces to the rack with the burgers. Place the rolls, cut-sides down, in the skillet and cook in the remaining butter until golden brown, about 1 minute.

Place 2 tablespoons of hollandaise on the bottom half of each roll and top with 2 pieces of the asparagus. Top with a lettuce leaf, a burger, and a piece of lobster tail. Close with the top buns and serve immediately.

Ultimate Veggie Burgers

Serves 4

Packed with basically the entire contents of a health food store, these veggie burgers are full of protein from quinoa, chickpeas, and black beans. The sautéed carrots and zucchini not only add color, but also keep the burgers from drying out.

4 tablespoons olive oil

1 large carrot, coarsely grated

1 medium zucchini, coarsely grated

½ small red onion, minced

Kosher salt and freshly ground black pepper

4 scallions, thinly sliced

1 cup cooked bulgur

1 cup cooked quinoa

1 cup canned chickpeas, drained and rinsed

1 cup canned black beans, drained and rinsed

2 tablespoons fresh lemon juice

1 teaspoon ground cumin

Large handful of fresh parsley leaves, coarsely chopped

4 multigrain hamburger buns

½ cup mayonnaise

4 large Bibb lettuce leaves

4 slices jalapeño cheddar cheese (or pepper Jack cheese)

1 large heirloom tomato, thinly sliced

Place 2 tablespoons of the olive oil in a large nonstick skillet set over medium-high heat. Add the carrot, zucchini, and onion and season with a large pinch of salt and a few grinds of pepper. Cook, stirring, until the vegetables are just tender but still have some crunch, about 4 minutes. Transfer the vegetables to a large bowl; set the skillet aside (no need to wash it). Add the scallions and bulgur to the bowl and set aside.

Place the quinoa, chickpeas, black beans, lemon juice, cumin, parsley, and 1 teaspoon salt in a food processor and pulse until the fixture comes together almost like a dough (you will need just three or four pulses—do not overprocess). Transfer the mixture to the bowl of vegetables and mix everything together well with your hands. Divide the mixture into 4 even patties.

Place the remaining 2 tablespoons olive oil in the skillet you used for the vegetables and set it over medium-high heat. Place the burgers in the skillet and cook until nicely browned on both sides, about 2 minutes per side.

Spread the cut sides of the buns with the mayonnaise and place a piece of lettuce on the bottom half of each bun. Place a burger and a slice of cheese on top of each piece of lettuce. Divide the tomatoes among the burgers and close the burgers with the top buns. Serve immediately.

Grilled Flank Steak Sandwiches with Horseradish Sauce

Serves 4

The only thing we love more than a perfectly grilled steak is slicing one and piling it on a roll with creamy horseradish sauce and a handful of peppery arugula. The squeeze of lemon on the greens might seem easy to skip, but it's essential. It sort of wakes up all the heavy flavors and makes all the difference.

1 small flank steak (about 1½ pounds), at room temperature

2 tablespoons JWB Steak Seasoning (page 171), or 2 teaspoons kosher salt plus 1 teaspoon freshly ground black pepper

2 tablespoons neutral oil (such as canola or vegetable)

½ cup mayonnaise

1 tablespoon Dijon mustard

3 tablespoons prepared horseradish

½ teaspoon kosher salt

4 kaiser rolls, split and lightly toasted

4 small handfuls of baby arugula

½ lemon

Preheat an outdoor grill to high or set a grill pan over high heat.

Season the steak on both sides with the steak seasoning.

Grill the steak, turning it a few times while it's cooking, until nicely charred on both sides and just firm to the touch, about 5 minutes per side (if you like it rare, take it off after 3 minutes on each side; you can leave it on longer, of course, if you prefer it more well done). Transfer the steak to a cutting board and let it rest for at least 15 minutes before slicing.

Meanwhile, place the mayonnaise, mustard, horseradish, and salt in a small bowl and whisk together. Evenly divide the mayonnaise mixture among the toasted rolls.

Thinly slice the steak across the grain and divide it among the bottom halves of the rolls. Evenly divide the arugula among the sandwiches and squeeze a little juice from the lemon half over each one. Close the sandwiches, cut each one in half, and serve immediately.

Cuban Meat Loaf
Survival Sandwiches

Serves 4

"I have stuffed many of these tasty treats into the Igloo cooler of my flats skiff as I head out for a day of fishing," says Jimmy. This sandwich, based on an old Key West recipe, consists of a Cuban roll filled with homemade meat loaf, cheddar cheese, shredded lettuce, tomatoes, and grilled onions. Why the name? According to Jimmy, "It doubles as a great lunch or a gourmet survival meal if you get washed out to sea for some strange reason." While we recommend a long day on a fishing boat to get the true experience of this sandwich, it's not integral to the recipe. Just try to eat it somewhere where you're totally relaxed. Cuban-style sandwich rolls, or *bolillos*, are often available in the bread bins at large supermarkets and are always available at Latin markets.

1 large yellow onion, cut into thick rings

2 tablespoons olive oil

4 Cuban-style sandwich rolls (bolillos), split

½ cup yellow mustard

8 slices cheddar cheese

2 cups shredded iceberg lettuce

8 large tomato slices

4 large slices Margaritaville Family Recipe Cuban Meat Loaf (page 167)

Preheat an outdoor grill to high or set a grill pan over high heat. Coat the onion rings with the oil and grill, turning now and then, until softened and browned, about 10 minutes. Set aside.

Evenly spread the mustard over the cut sides of the rolls. Divide the cheese, lettuce, tomatoes, meat loaf, and grilled onions among the rolls. Serve immediately or wrap them up and take them to go.

A Day on the Beach

Tailgate Muffuletta for a Crowd

Serves 6

During one of Jimmy's visits to the New Orleans Margaritaville Café, he suggested a walk up the street to Central Grocery, home of the muffuletta, to pick up some of the famous sandwiches for the café's staff. There was a long line to purchase the room-temperature, deli paper–wrapped sandwiches that were stacked tall behind the counter, but they were well worth the wait. The restaurant team was hooked at first bite and immediately set out to replicate this New Orleans standard as an homage to the original. It became a mainstay on the menu for many years. We love it for tailgates or picnics, since one sandwich serves a ton of people and it doesn't suffer if it sits for a while.

1 celery stalk, finely diced

3 tablespoons minced red onion

1 garlic clove, minced

1 jarred roasted red bell pepper, finely diced

½ cup mixed pitted olives, finely chopped

1 tablespoon drained capers

¼ cup red wine vinegar

¼ cup olive oil

1 tablespoon dried oregano

1 large loaf seeded Italian bread (about 1½ pounds), round if you can find it, split

¼ pound thinly sliced salami

¼ pound thinly sliced prosciutto

¼ pound thinly sliced mortadella

¼ pound thinly sliced provolone cheese

½ pound ounces fresh mozzarella, thinly sliced

Place the celery, onion, garlic, roasted pepper, olives, capers, vinegar, olive oil, and oregano in a medium bowl and stir well to combine.

Spread the olive salad evenly over the cut sides of the bread. Layer on the salami, prosciutto, mortadella, provolone, and mozzarella. Close the sandwich and wrap it tightly in plastic wrap. Place a baking sheet on top of the sandwich and place something heavy (like a cast-iron skillet or a few cans of tomatoes) on top of the baking sheet. Let the sandwich sit for at least 1 hour. Slice the sandwich into individual portions and serve.

Beach Club Sandwich

Makes 1, easily multiplied

The only difference between a regular club sandwich and a beach club sandwich is that the latter is eaten on a towel or a lounge chair, preferably with your toes in the sand and a frosty drink next to you. Here is our favorite double-decker club sandwich filled with turkey, Swiss, bacon, and ham. While the beach part is optional, we highly recommend it.

2 tablespoons mayonnaise

1 tablespoon Dijon mustard

3 slices country white bread, lightly toasted

2 slices deli turkey

2 slices Swiss cheese

½ cup shredded iceberg lettuce

2 slices bacon, cooked until crisp and cut in half

2 slices fresh tomato

2 slices deli ham

Place the mayonnaise and mustard in a small bowl and stir together. Spread the mixture over one side of each piece of toast, end to end, dividing it evenly.

Place the turkey, Swiss cheese, and half the lettuce on the mayonnaise-spread side of one piece of toast. Top with another slice of toast, mayonnaise facing up. Top with the bacon, tomatoes, remaining lettuce, and ham. Top that with the final piece of toast, mayonnaise side facing down. Push two skewers into opposing corners of the sandwich and slice the sandwich in half in between the skewers (this way, the skewers help hold the halves together). Serve immediately.

New Orleans Fried Oyster Po'Boys

Serves 4

Whenever Jimmy would stop by our café in New Orleans, his visits would invariably include a fried oyster po'boy fully dressed (meaning with mayo, pickles, and shredded lettuce, all doused with hot sauce). A funny story: Jimmy is a big Phish fan, and when Phish played Jazz Fest for the first time back in 1999, Jimmy invited the band to come by his post-fairgrounds show at the Margaritaville Café. The restaurant staff had to break the news to Jimmy and Phish that no po'boys were available because all the French bread in the French Quarter had vanished. At that time, the Gambino's and Leidenheimer bakeries supplied the bread for our po'boys, and pretty much everyone else's in the neighborhood, and their trucks made very early morning routes through the French Quarter. They would leave bags of bread at the back doors of the restaurants and bars for the chefs to bring inside. On that particular day, after a night of partying on limited budgets, the roving packs of Phishheads followed the trucks along their routes, picking up the bags of French bread for a "free" continental breakfast.

24 oysters, shucked, half of the shells reserved

1 cup whole milk

1 cup all-purpose flour

1 cup finely ground cornmeal

3 tablespoons cornstarch

1 teaspoon kosher salt, plus more for sprinkling

Neutral oil (such as canola or vegetable), for frying

1 cup mayonnaise

4 individual-size loaves French bread, split

1 cup shredded iceberg lettuce

2 large dill pickles, diced

Place the shucked oysters and milk in a large bowl and mix well.

Place the flour, cornmeal, cornstarch, and salt in a separate medium bowl and whisk together.

Lift the oysters from the milk (discard the milk) and place them in the flour mixture. Coat each oyster well. Shake off the excess flour.

Meanwhile, pour 1 inch of oil into a large heavy pot and heat the oil over medium heat. Test the oil: When a pinch of the flour mixture sizzles upon contact, it's ready. Add the dredged oysters to the hot oil, working in batches as necessary so that the oysters don't crowd the pot. Cook, turning the oysters a few times while they cook, until browned all over, about 3 minutes. Transfer the fried oysters to a paper towel–lined plate and fry the remaining oysters.

Meanwhile, spread the mayonnaise over the cut sides of each loaf of bread, dividing it evenly. Divide the lettuce, pickles, and hot fried oysters among the loaves. Serve immediately.

Delta Fried Catfish Reubens

Serves 4

An unlikely fusion of a classic Reuben and a fried fish sandwich, it was originally served with a single fried catfish filet. Once on a stop-in during Jazz Fest, Jimmy suggested we travel across the border to Trapani's Eatery in Bay St. Louis to experience their thin-sliced fried catfish (Trapani's catered the "Bama Breeze" video shoot in Mississippi in 2006). Enlightened, we changed our catfish preparation to the wafer-thin crispy planks perfected by the Trapani family.

1 cup buttermilk

1 tablespoon hot sauce

Four 6-ounce pieces catfish or other firm white-fleshed fish such as mahi-mahi or grouper, thinly sliced

½ cup all-purpose flour

½ cup cornmeal

1 teaspoon paprika

1 teaspoon freshly ground black pepper

1 teaspoon kosher salt

2 teaspoons garlic powder

Neutral oil (such as canola or vegetable), for frying

4 tablespoons (½ stick) unsalted butter, softened

8 thick slices white bread

½ cup Paradise Island Dressing (page 129) or store-bought Thousand Island dressing

8 slices Swiss cheese

½ cup good-quality sauerkraut

Place the buttermilk and hot sauce in a large bowl and whisk together. Add the fish and turn the pieces to coat them well.

Place the flour, cornmeal, paprika, pepper, salt, and garlic powder in a separate bowl.

Lift the fish from the buttermilk (discard the buttermilk) and place it in the flour mixture. Coat each piece well.

Meanwhile, pour 1 inch of oil into a large heavy pot and heat the oil over medium heat. Test the oil: When a pinch of the flour mixture sizzles upon contact, it's ready. Carefully place the fish into the hot oil, spacing the pieces evenly so they don't touch (work in batches if necessary). Cook the fish, turning the pieces once while they cook, until golden brown all over, about 6 minutes. Transfer the fish to a paper towel–lined plate to drain while you prepare the bread.

Place the butter on a nonstick griddle over medium-high heat (or set up two large nonstick pans). Place the bread on the griddle. While the undersides brown, work quickly to spread 1 tablespoon of the Paradise Island Dressing on the unbuttered side (the side facing you) of each slice and top each with a piece of Swiss cheese. Divide the fried fish among four slices of bread and top each with 2 tablespoons of the sauerkraut. When the cheese has melted, close the sandwiches and transfer them to a cutting board. Cut each sandwich in half (we do it on the diagonal) and serve immediately.

Blackened Fish Sandwiches

Serves 4

We've had a simple fish sandwich on all our menus since day one. This version might be our favorite of all time. It features blackened fish with our go-to mix of spices, plus spicy Jalapeño Tartar Sauce and Cilantro-Lime Coleslaw for both flavor and crunch. You could substitute plain grilled fish or fried fish (like the LandShark Beer–Battered Fish on page 217) for the blackened fish and any of our sauces if you don't like the kick of jalapeño.

Four 6-ounce pieces firm white-fleshed fish, such as mahimahi or grouper

4 teaspoons Blackening Seasoning (page 93)

2 tablespoons neutral oil (such as canola or vegetable)

½ cup Jalapeño Tartar Sauce (recipe follows)

4 brioche hamburger buns, split and lightly toasted

1 cup Cilantro-Lime Coleslaw (page 242)

2 medium yellow (or red) tomatoes, thinly sliced

Preheat the oven to 400°F.

Evenly sprinkle the blackening seasoning on all sides of the fish.

Place the oil in a medium cast-iron skillet set over medium-high heat. Once it's nice and hot, add the fish and cook, turning the pieces once, until well browned on both sides, about 2 minutes per side. Transfer the skillet to the oven and continue cooking the fish until it is firm to the touch and flakes easily when pushed with a fork or paring knife, about 5 minutes.

Spread the tartar sauce over the cut sides of the buns, dividing it evenly. Place a piece of fish on top of each one. Divide the coleslaw and tomatoes among the sandwiches and close each sandwich. Serve immediately.

Jalapeño Tartar Sauce

Both creamy and spicy, this tartar sauce really benefits from sitting for at least an hour before serving. That way, all the fresh jalapeño flavor can really announce itself and infuse the sauce. This is not only used on Blackened Fish Sandwiches (page 152), but also as a dip for LandShark Beer–Battered Fish (page 217), Oven Fries (page 254), and Spicy Red Onion Rings (page 246).

1 cup mayonnaise

2 tablespoons pickle relish

2 scallions, minced

1 tablespoon drained capers

1 jalapeño, seeded and minced

1 teaspoon dried dill

Place all the ingredients in a bowl and whisk together. Cover and refrigerate for at least 1 hour before serving or transfer to an airtight container and refrigerate for up to 1 week.

JWB Lobster Rolls

Serves 4

Simple lobster rolls depend on a few key details. The first is the simply dressed lobster that highlights the sandwich. The second is to toast the buns in butter, because if you're going to have a lobster roll, every single part of it should be as delicious as possible. Feel free to serve with a ramekin of extra melted butter for drizzling on top because why not? If you'd like a fun spin on lobster rolls, coat the lobster with the curry dressing from the Curry Kale Slaw (page 56).

Kosher salt

Two 1½ -pound lobsters

3 tablespoons unsalted butter

2 tablespoons fresh lemon juice

Small handful of fresh chives, minced

Small handful of fresh cilantro leaves, finely chopped

Pinch of cayenne pepper

4 hot dog buns, split

4 large Bibb lettuce leaves

2 lemons, halved crosswise

Bring a large pot of water to a boil and salt it generously. Add the lobsters and boil until they're bright red and the meat inside is cooked through, 8 minutes. Transfer the lobsters to a baking sheet and let them cool. Once they're cool enough to handle, break the lobsters down and pick the meat. Coarsely chop any large pieces (discard the shells or reserve them for making stock, page 118).

Place 2 tablespoons of the butter in a large nonstick skillet set over medium heat. Once it melts, add the lobster meat and cook, stirring, until it's barely warmed, about 30 seconds. Transfer the warm lobster to a large bowl and add the lemon juice, chives, cilantro, and cayenne and mix well to combine. Season the lobster with salt and set aside.

Place the remaining 1 tablespoon butter in the skillet. Once it melts, add the buns, cut-sides down, and cook until lightly browned, about 1 minute. Place a lettuce leaf in each bun and evenly divide the lobster among the buns. Serve immediately with the lemon halves for squeezing on top.

Aloha Hot Dogs

Topped with a punchy pineapple salsa, these hot dogs have all the flavor of Hawaii without the long airplane flight. Serve these with a refreshing pitcher of Frozen Watermelon and Mint Margaritas (page 311) for the adults and Watermelon Pink Lemonade (page 317) for the kids.

¼ cup mayonnaise

1 garlic clove, minced

2 teaspoons fresh lemon juice

Pinch of kosher salt

4 hot dogs

4 hot dog buns, split

¾ cup Pineapple Salsa (recipe follows)

Large handful of fresh cilantro leaves, for serving

Place the mayonnaise, garlic, lemon, and salt in a small bowl and whisk together. Set aside.

Preheat an outdoor grill to high or set a grill pan over high heat. Place the hot dogs on the grill and cook, turning them now and then, until browned all over, about 4 minutes. During the last minute of grilling, place the buns on the grill, cut-sides down, and grill until lightly browned and warmed through.

Spread the mayonnaise mixture over the cut sides of the buns, dividing it evenly. Place the hot dogs in the buns and top with the pineapple salsa and cilantro. Serve immediately.

Pineapple Salsa

With all of the flavors of Hawaii, this salsa is vital for the Aloha Hot Dogs (page 156), but it is also just a wonderful fresh salsa on its own. Serve with tortilla chips and margaritas or use it as an accompaniment on a piece of simple fish in the spirit of the Seared Grouper with Fresh Mango Salsa (page 206).

2 cups finely diced fresh pineapple

½ jalapeño, seeded and minced

1 teaspoon minced fresh ginger

1 small garlic clove, minced

Small handful of fresh cilantro leaves, finely chopped

¼ teaspoon kosher salt

3 tablespoons fresh lime juice

Place all the ingredients in a bowl and stir together. Serve immediately or store in an airtight container in the fridge for up to 3 days.

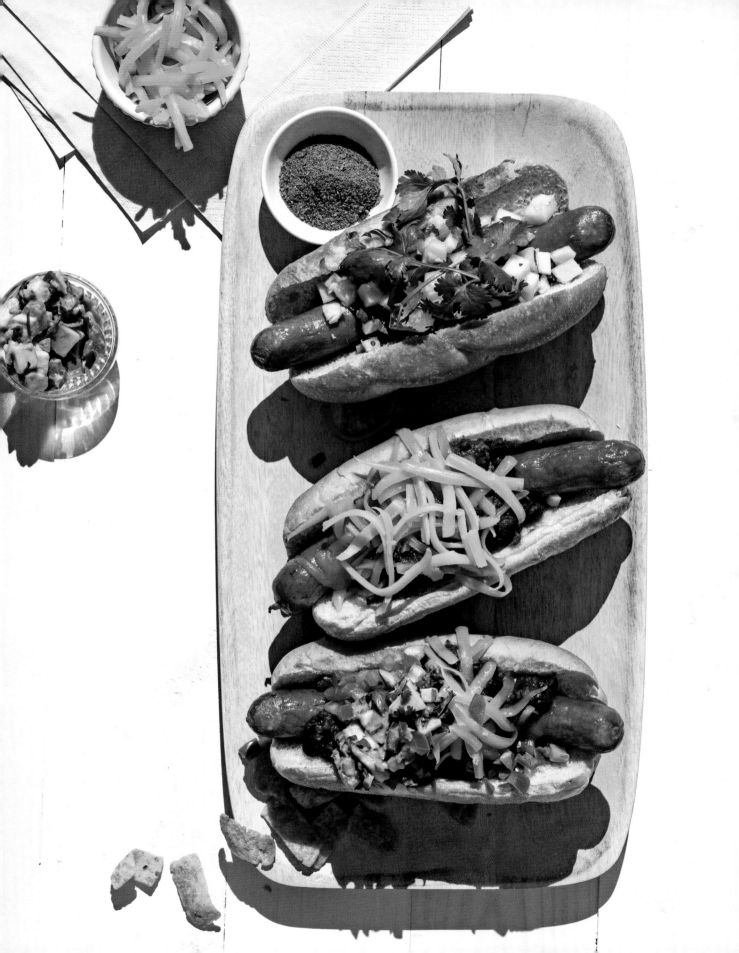

Own-Damn-Fault Hot Dogs

Serves 4

Named for the lyric in the song "Margaritaville," these hot dogs combine all the familiar flavors of chili cheese dogs with our favorite Mexican condiments, including fresh pico de gallo, creamy guacamole, spicy jalapeños, and crunchy corn chips. It's really fun to put all the toppings out in bowls and let everyone build their own.

4 hot dogs

4 hot dog buns, split

1 cup Best-Ever Chili (page 164), warm

½ cup coarsely grated cheddar cheese

½ cup Pico de Gallo (page 238) or your favorite salsa

½ cup Guacamole (page 241)

1 jalapeño, seeded and finely diced

½ cup corn chips (preferably Fritos)

Preheat an outdoor grill to high or set a grill pan over high heat. Place the dogs on the grill and cook, turning them now and then, until browned all over, about 4 minutes. During the last minute of grilling, place the buns on the grill, cut-sides down, and grill until lightly browned and warmed through.

Place the hot dogs in the buns and top with the chili, cheese, pico de gallo, guacamole, jalapeño, and corn chips. Serve immediately.

Blackened Chili Dogs

Serves 4

Featured on our original Key West menu, these hot dogs take old-fashioned chili cheese dogs up a notch with our signature blackening seasoning mix and our Best-Ever Chili. If you'd like, run the dressed hot dogs under the broiler to melt the cheese.

4 teaspoons Blackening Seasoning (page 93)

4 hot dogs

4 hot dog buns, split

1 cup Best-Ever Chili (page 164), warm

½ cup coarsely grated cheddar cheese

Preheat an outdoor grill to high or set a grill pan over high heat. Season the hot dogs all over with the blackening seasoning, put them on the grill, and cook, turning them now and then, until browned all over, about 4 minutes. During the last minute of grilling, place the buns on the grill, cut-sides down, and grill until lightly browned and warmed through.

Place the hot dogs in the buns and top with the chili and cheese. Serve immediately.

Main
Dishes

"I SAVOR THE SCENT OF THE FISH ON THE GRILL, LIFE'S SO SPICY UP ON BAR-B-Q HILL...."

These main dishes are bound to become part of your regular family repertoire. If you need something cozy to enjoy at the kitchen table, there's homey food like our Best-Ever Chili (page 164) and Margaritaville Family Recipe Cuban Meat Loaf (page 167). Or for a dinner party in the dining room (with real napkins!), there's also more elevated food that sounds complicated but couldn't be easier to make, like Seared Grouper with Fresh Mango Salsa (page 206). In addition, you'll find our most trusted recipes for parties and crowds, like the Outside-Optional Cajun Clambake (page 199) and Baby Back Ribs with Guava Barbecue Sauce (page 228). The biggest showstopper is the Paella del Mar (page 222), which Carlo learned to make from a chef who used to cook for Spanish royalty. And for one of the best one-pot meals around, there's Jimmy's Jammin' Jambalaya (page 225) which needs nothing more than a table of friends and a bottle of hot sauce.

Best-Ever Chili

Serves 4

The centerpiece of our Volcano Nachos (page 36), this chili can also be served on its own, topped with sour cream and grated cheese, maybe some sliced scallions and/or pickled jalapeños, lime wedges, and fresh cilantro or parsley. Just don't forget the Skillet Cornbread with Honey Butter (page 260), aka chili's best friend. For a completely vegan version, omit the beef and add two extra cans of beans (black beans, kidney beans, and/or black-eyed peas all work especially well).

2 tablespoons neutral oil (such as canola or vegetable)

1 pound ground beef

Kosher salt

1 small red onion, finely diced

1 green bell pepper, finely diced

3 garlic cloves, minced

½ cup tomato paste

2 tablespoons dried red chile powder

1½ tablespoons ground cumin

1 teaspoon dried oregano

Pinch of cayenne pepper

A few grinds of black pepper

A few dashes of hot sauce

One 14.5-ounce can diced tomatoes, undrained

One 15-ounce can black beans, undrained

Place 1 tablespoon of the oil in a large heavy pot set over medium-high heat. Add the beef and season aggressively with salt. Cook, stirring now and then, until the meat has released its liquid and that liquid has evaporated and the meat is well browned, about 15 minutes. Using a slotted spoon, transfer the beef to a bowl and set aside. Add the remaining 1 tablespoon oil to the pot. Add the onion and bell pepper and season aggressively with salt. Cook, stirring now and then, until the vegetables are browned and the edges are softened, about 10 minutes.

Add the garlic, tomato paste, chile powder, cumin, oregano, cayenne, black pepper, hot sauce, diced tomatoes (with their liquid), black beans (with their liquid), and the cooked beef. Sprinkle everything with a few pinches of salt and give the whole thing a good stir to make sure the tomato paste is incorporated. Bring the mixture to a boil, reduce the heat to maintain a simmer, and partially cover the pot. Simmer the chili, uncovering to stir it now and then, until all the flavors are well combined and it's nice and thick, about 30 minutes. Taste and season one final time with salt and/or more hot sauce if needed. Serve hot.

Margaritaville Family Recipe
Cuban Meat Loaf

Serves 6

The mix of roasted garlic, cumin, mustard, and cilantro gives this meat loaf a Cuban edge. We make it all the time to use for Cuban Meat Loaf Survival Sandwiches (page 140), but it can also stand on its own as an entrée. It pairs especially well with Cilantro-Lime Coleslaw (page 242) and Yukon Gold Loaded Mashed Potatoes (page 245).

12 garlic cloves, peeled and left whole

1 teaspoon olive oil

2 teaspoons kosher salt

½ teaspoon freshly ground black pepper

2 teaspoons ground cumin

2 teaspoons chile powder

3 tablespoons yellow mustard

Large handful of fresh cilantro leaves, finely chopped

2 large eggs, lightly beaten

½ small red onion, finely diced

½ green bell pepper, finely diced

1 pound ground beef

1 pound ground pork

½ cup plain bread crumbs

Preheat the oven to 350°F. Line a baking sheet with parchment paper.

Place the garlic cloves on a double layer of aluminum foil and drizzle with the olive oil. Use your hands to make sure all the garlic cloves are evenly coated. Wrap the garlic in the foil and roast until the cloves are softened, about 20 minutes.

Unwrap the garlic and mash it to a paste with a fork. Transfer the roasted garlic paste to a large bowl and add the salt, black pepper, cumin, chile powder, yellow mustard, cilantro, eggs, onions, and bell pepper. Stir everything together until evenly combined. Add the beef, pork, and bread crumbs and use your clean hands (they're the best tool for the job) to mix everything together.

Transfer the meat loaf mixture to the parchment-lined baking sheet. Shape the mixture into a rectangular loaf that measures about 10 inches by 5 inches and is about 2 inches high. Bake the meat loaf until browned and firm to the touch and a meat thermometer inserted into the center registers 160°F, about 55 minutes. Let the meat loaf rest for at least 10 minutes before slicing and serving warm. Or, of course, let it cool to room temperature (or wrap it in plastic and refrigerate for up to 4 days) and use it for Cuban Meat Loaf Survival Sandwiches.

Veal Saltimbocca Pockets

Serves 4

Taking inspiration from Carlo's Italian upbringing, this veal dish is a very fun interpretation of traditional *saltimbocca alla Romana*. Filled with Parmesan, sage, and prosciutto, it's become one of our most special specials at JWB. If you'd like, fry some extra sage leaves in a small skillet of hot olive oil to garnish the dish. We serve it with a simple green salad and roasted potatoes and suggest you do the same at home to make a memorable dinner. Speaking of veal, Carlo's other favorite way to enjoy it is a Milanese sandwich. Just bread paper-thin veal cutlets and shallow-fry them (just like the eggplant on page 80), then place on halved baguettes that you've spread with lots of mayonnaise and top with fresh mozzarella and arugula. Bring on the boat picnic!

1 pound veal sirloin or rump steak (any cut from the hip), cut into 8 thin slices

About 1¼ cups olive oil

3 tablespoons fresh lemon juice

1 teaspoon kosher salt

2 cups finely grated Parmesan cheese

2 cups fine bread crumbs

8 large fresh sage leaves

8 thin slices prosciutto

Preheat the oven to 400°F.

Brush two large pieces of parchment paper with a little olive oil (about 1 tablespoon each) and place a veal slice on top of one. Place the second parchment piece, oil-side down, on top of the veal. Use a meat pounder to delicately and evenly pound the veal so that it's ¼ inch thick. Repeat the process, re-oiling the parchment as needed, with the rest of the veal.

Place 1 cup of the olive oil, the lemon juice, and the salt in a large bowl and whisk together. Place the veal slices in the bowl and mix well to make sure they are all coated. Let the pieces marinate for a few minutes while you prepare your breading station.

Meanwhile, place the Parmesan in a shallow baking dish or on a large plate and place the bread crumbs in another. Working with one slice of veal at a time, lift it out of the olive oil mixture and rub it against the side of the bowl so that the extra oil drips back into the bowl. Lay the veal on the Parmesan, pressing it down firmly so that the underside gets completely coated with cheese. Flip

(continued)

the veal over and press it down in the bread crumbs so that the second side gets coated with bread crumbs. While the veal is lying in the bread crumbs, place a sage leaf and a slice of prosciutto on the Parmesan-coated side of the veal and fold the veal over itself to form a pocket (now the entire piece should be coated with bread crumbs and the cheese, sage, and prosciutto should be safely enclosed inside). Repeat the process with the remaining pieces of veal, sage, and prosciutto.

Place the remaining 2 tablespoons olive oil in a large nonstick skillet set over medium-high heat. Once it's nice and hot, place the veal pockets in the skillet, working in batches as necessary so that you don't crowd the skillet, and cook until the bottoms are golden brown, about 2 minutes. Carefully turn the pockets over and let them cook until the second side is golden brown, about 2 minutes more.

Transfer the browned pockets to a baking sheet and evenly space them apart. Roast the pockets until firm to the touch, about 5 minutes. Serve the veal pockets immediately while they're hot and crispy.

JWB Steak Seasoning

Can you keep one of Carlo's secrets? The flavor that makes our steak seasoning so special is ground dried porcini mushrooms. They can be a little pricey, but a few go a very long way. Mixed with salt and pepper, the ground mushrooms are basically the personification of umami (the Japanese word that roughly translates to "savory flavor"). Similar to highly flavorful things like ketchup and Parmesan, the porcini mushrooms turn up the volume on whatever you combine them with. We find that they make steaks taste even beefier and more like themselves.

1 ounce dried porcini mushrooms

2 tablespoons whole black peppercorns

¼ cup kosher salt

Place the mushrooms and peppercorns in a clean coffee grinder and grind until fine. Transfer the mixture to a bowl and whisk in the salt. Store the seasoning in a closed container in a dark spot at room temperature for up to 2 months.

Prime Sirloin Oscar

At JWB, seafood is just as important as steak (just ask Carlo, who is equally happy in the water as he is in the kitchen). Needless to say, we like a lot of surf with our turf, and this Sirloin Oscar is one of our bestselling dishes. It features a prime steak that's topped with lots of fresh, jumbo lump crabmeat and luscious Key Lime Hollandaise. At the restaurant, we serve this with Yukon Gold Loaded Mashed Potatoes (page 245) and simple grilled asparagus, which we highly recommend for a complete, very hearty meal.

Four 12-ounce prime sirloin steaks, at room temperature

2 tablespoons JWB Steak Seasoning (page 171), or 2 teaspoons kosher salt plus 1 teaspoon freshly ground black pepper

2 tablespoons neutral oil (such as canola or vegetable)

1 tablespoon flaky sea salt (such as Maldon)

½ pound fresh or pasteurized jumbo lump crabmeat

2 teaspoons finely grated lemon zest

1 tablespoon fresh lemon juice

1 tablespoon olive oil

½ teaspoon kosher salt

1 teaspoon dried red chile powder

1 cup Key Lime Hollandaise (page 20), warmed

Mircrogreens or minced fresh chives, for serving

Preheat the broiler to high. Position the rack so it's about 6 inches from the heating element. Let the broiler heat until it's super hot, at least 10 minutes.

Season the steaks on both sides with the steak seasoning.

Place the oil in a large heavy cast-iron skillet that can hold the steaks in a single layer (or work in batches or use two skillets). Set the skillet over high heat and turn your exhaust fan on. Once the skillet is smoking hot, place the steaks in the skillet and cook until the bottoms are nicely browned, about 2 minutes. Carefully turn the steaks and cook until the second side is nicely browned, 2 minutes more.

Place the skillet under the broiler and cook until the steaks are done to your liking (depending on the thickness of your steaks and strength of your broiler, it will take about 2 minutes for medium-rare, 4 minutes for medium, and 6 minutes for well-done).

Transfer the steaks to a wire rack set over a baking sheet (to collect any juices) and let rest for at least 10 minutes before serving. Sprinkle the flaky salt evenly over the steaks.

While the steaks rest, place the crabmeat, lemon zest, lemon juice, olive oil, kosher salt, and chile powder in a large bowl. Stir gently to combine (you want to preserve some nice big pieces of crab).

Place a steak on each of four warm dinner plates. Divide the hollandaise and crab mixture between the steaks. Sprinkle each with microgreens (or chives) and serve immediately.

Steak au Poivre

With a traditional steak dish like steak au poivre, it's as much about the sauce as it is about the meat. With tons of assertive green peppercorns and plenty of mustard and brandy, our version is best prepared for those who like a kick. Serve these steaks with baked potatoes and JWB Creamed Spinach (page 253) for the most classic of steakhouse meals.

¾ cup drained green peppercorns in brine

Four 8-ounce prime tenderloin steaks (filet mignon), at room temperature

Kosher salt and freshly ground black pepper

½ cup all-purpose flour

4 tablespoons (½ stick) unsalted butter

2 tablespoons olive oil

¼ cup Dijon mustard

2 tablespoons coarse sugar (preferably turbinado) or granulated sugar

2 cups heavy cream

2 teaspoons green peppercorn brine

1⅓ cups brandy

Large handful of fresh parsley leaves, coarsely chopped

Preheat the oven to 425°F.

Place the green peppercorns in a resealable plastic bag and use a meat pounder to lightly pound them. You want to break them but not smash them completely. Set aside.

Season the steaks aggressively on both sides with salt and black pepper and lightly dust them with the flour (discard any excess flour).

Place 2 tablespoons of the butter and the olive oil in a large heavy skillet set over high heat. When the fat is nearly smoking, add the steaks (work in batches as necessary) and cook until nicely browned on both sides, 2 to 3 minutes per side. Transfer the steaks and their cooking juices to a baking sheet and set aside.

Place the remaining 2 tablespoons butter in the same pan. Once it melts, add the reserved mustard, sugar, cream, peppercorn brine, and brandy. Bring the mixture to a boil and cook, stirring, for 15 seconds, then reduce the heat to low. Add the juices from the plate the steaks are resting on. Season the sauce with salt and keep it warm over low heat.

Place the steaks in the oven and cook until they're cooked to your liking (about 2 minutes for medium-rare, 4 minutes for medium, and 6 minutes for well-done).

Transfer the steaks to serving plates and spoon over the sauce. Sprinkle with the parsley and serve immediately.

Summer Grill Surf 'n' Turf

We love treating really high-quality ingredients like steaks and lobster with lots of respect and zero pretension. The secret here is the sauce. Made from the juice of grilled lemons, which gets sweet and smoky, mixed with butter and garlic, it's so simple but so incredibly good and is the perfect complement to both the steak and the lobster.

4 Maine lobster tails

Four 8-ounce prime tenderloin steaks (filet mignon), at room temperature

2 tablespoons JWB Steak Seasoning (page 171), or 2 teaspoons kosher salt plus 1 teaspoon freshly ground black pepper

Neutral oil (such as canola or vegetable)

2 lemons, halved

6 tablespoons (½ stick) unsalted butter, melted

1 garlic clove, minced

1 teaspoon kosher salt

Large handful of dandelion greens (or baby arugula)

Preheat an outdoor grill to high or set a grill pan over high heat.

While the grill is heating, use a sharp knife to cut the lobster tails lengthwise on the top, rounded side of each tail, starting from the top where it connected to the body and working down to the tail end. Cut just to split the shell, not all the way through the meat. Use your hands to pop the meat out of the shells so that it's exposed (almost like you would pop open a baked potato). Alternatively, you can split the lobster tails lengthwise all the way through the meat.

Evenly sprinkle the steaks with the steak seasoning on both sides.

Once the grill is nice and hot, make sure the grates are very clean. Fold a paper towel a few times to form a small rectangle and pour a bit of oil onto it. Use tongs to grip the oiled paper towel and rub it on the grill grates.

Place the lobster tails, flesh-side down, and steaks on the grill along with the lemon halves, cut-side down. Grill the lemons only on the cut side and remove them from the grill when they're nicely charred, about 5 minutes. Grill the lobster tails and steaks, turning now and then, until slightly charred on both sides and just firm to the touch, about 8 minutes for the lobster tails and 12 minutes for steaks. Transfer the lobster tails and steaks to a platter to rest.

Squeeze the juice from the charred lemons into a large bowl and add the butter, garlic, and salt. Whisk everything together.

Add the greens to the platter, drizzle the butter mixture over everything, and serve warm.

Grilled Skirt Steaks with Carlo's Chimichurri

Serves 4

Essentially Argentinean pesto, chimichurri is an easy sauce made of chopped fresh herbs, oil, and garlic. Some folks like marinating meat in chimichurri, but we prefer to just spoon it on top so it doesn't lose any of its fresh, bright flavor. Try it on grilled chicken or fish, too. Serve with Cilantro-Lime Coleslaw (page 242) and fresh avocado for a simple, beautiful meal.

2 tablespoons neutral oil (such as canola or vegetable), plus more as needed

¼ cup dry white wine

1 teaspoon red pepper flakes or hot sauce

½ teaspoon kosher salt

½ teaspoon freshly ground black pepper

½ cup finely chopped fresh parsley

¼ cup finely chopped fresh cilantro

4 scallions, thinly sliced

1 garlic clove, minced

½ teaspoon dried oregano

2 pounds skirt steak

2 tablespoons JWB Steak Seasoning (page 171), or 2 teaspoons kosher salt plus 1 teaspoon freshly ground black pepper

Place the oil, wine, red pepper flakes, salt, black pepper, parsley, cilantro, scallions, garlic, and oregano in a food processor and pulse until relatively smooth. Set the chimichurri aside.

Preheat an outdoor grill to high or set a grill pan over high heat. Make sure the grates are very clean. Fold a paper towel a few times to form a small rectangle and pour a bit of oil onto it. Use tongs to grip the oiled paper towel and rub it on the grill grates.

Evenly sprinkle the steak with the steak seasoning on both side and place it on the grill. Grill the steak, turning now and then, until slightly charred on both sides and just firm to the touch, about 8 minutes. Transfer the steak to a cutting board and allow it to rest for at least 10 minutes.

Slice the steak across the grain as thick or as thin as you like and transfer to a platter. Serve warm, with the chimichurri on top or alongside.

Slow Cooker Pork Shoulder with LandShark and Cola

Serves 10

You can set this pork up early in the morning and have the most wonderful meal waiting for you by dinnertime. Perfect for tailgating or when you have friends over to watch a game, this slowly cooked pork can be served on its own with rice and beans and is also amazing as a taco or sandwich filling. Serve with sandwich rolls and slaw, or with tortillas alongside bowls of fresh cilantro, scallions (raw, grilled, or roasted), crumbled cotija cheese, sour cream, and Salsa Verde (page 187) for everyone to mix and match. Round out the build-your-own meal with a platter of Grilled Corn with Lime Butter (page 263). If you don't have a slow cooker, simply follow the same instructions for cooking the pork but use a large roasting pan or a large pot, cover it tightly, and cook the pork in a 300°F oven until tender, about 5 hours. For an extra layer of flavor, raise the oven temperature to 450°F and brown the pork for 15 minutes on either side before shredding.

3 cups beer (preferably LandShark Lager)

½ cup cola soda (not diet)

3 garlic cloves, minced

2 tablespoons distilled white vinegar

3 teaspoons kosher salt

2 teaspoons freshly ground black pepper

2 teaspoons chipotle chile powder or dried red chile powder)

1 bone-in pork shoulder (about 8 pounds)

2 medium red onions, coarsely chopped

1 bunch fresh thyme

2 teaspoons hot sauce (preferably Tabasco)

3 tablespoons fresh lime juice

Place 2 cups of the beer, the cola, garlic, vinegar, 2 teaspoons of the salt, 1 teaspoon of the pepper, and 1 teaspoon of the chile powder in a large bowl and whisk together. Transfer the mixture to a large resealable plastic bag and add the pork and onions, making sure the entire piece of meat is in contact with the beer mixture. Seal the bag and refrigerate, turning the bag at least once, for 12 hours. Take the bag out of the fridge an hour before you're ready to cook.

(continued)

Place the onions from the bag in the bottom of your slow cooker and top with half the thyme. Place the pork, fat-side up, on top of the thyme and pour over the marinade plus the remaining 1 cup beer. Season the top of the pork with the remaining 1 teaspoon each salt, pepper, and chile powder. Place the remaining thyme on top. Cover and cook on low until incredibly tender, 10 hours. Transfer the pork to a work surface to rest. Pick out and discard the thyme stems (pretty much all the leaves will have fallen off). Once the pork is cool enough to handle, shred the meat with your hands and discard any large pieces of fat and the bone. Return the shredded meat to the slow cooker and drizzle with the hot sauce and lime juice. Mix the meat into its cooking juices. Season with additional salt and pepper if needed.

Chicken Enchiladas with Salsa Verde and Smoked Ancho and Pasilla Sauce

These require a few components, but the sum of the parts are truly the best enchiladas in the world. Each component, from the Chicken Tinga (page 189) to the simple Salsa Verde (page 187) and the Smoked Ancho and Pasilla Sauce (page 186) can all have lives on their own (there are notes for all these on their respective recipes). Don't skip the quick frying of the tortillas. It helps to keep them from disintegrating as they bake.

2 cups fresh corn kernels

1 recipe Salsa Verde (page 187)

¼ cup neutral oil (such as canola or vegetable)

12 corn tortillas (preferably fresh white corn tortillas)

1 cup Smoked Ancho and Pasilla Sauce (page 186)

1 recipe Chicken Tinga (page 189)

2 large handfuls of fresh cilantro (tender stems included), coarsely chopped

1½ cups coarsely grated Monterey Jack or mozzarella cheese

½ cup mayonnaise

2 tablespoons fresh lime juice

2 tablespoons chile paste (preferably ají amarillo chile paste)

½ teaspoon kosher salt

4 radishes, thinly sliced

Large handful of crumbled queso fresco

Preheat the oven to 400°F.

Place the corn kernels in a small cast iron skillet and place in the oven. Roast the corn, stirring now and then, until charred in spots, about 15 minutes. Reserve the corn.

Pour half the salsa verde over the bottom of a 9 x 13-inch baking dish. Spread the sauce to cover.

Place the canola oil in a large nonstick skillet set over medium-high heat. Working in batches, fry the tortillas until softened and pliable, about 15 seconds per side. Place the Smoked Ancho and Pasilla Sauce in a large bowl and dip the tortillas in it to coat them on both sides. You should use pretty much all the sauce. Any extra can be stirred into the Chicken Tinga.

Transfer the fried and sauced tortillas to a work surface and divide the Chicken Tinga, reserved corn, and a handful of the chopped cilantro among them. Roll the tortillas tightly around the filling and line them up in the baking dish, seam-side down. Pour the remaining salsa verde over the tortillas and sprinkle evenly with the Monterey Jack.

Bake the enchiladas until the cheese is melted and golden brown and the sauce is bubbling, about 10 minutes.

Meanwhile, place the mayonnaise, lime juice, chile paste, and salt in a small bowl and whisk together. Drizzle the mixture over the enchiladas (or serve alongside) and sprinkle the enchiladas with the radishes, queso fresco, and remaining cilantro. Serve immediately.

Smoked Ancho and Pasilla Sauce

Makes about 4 cups

Although it requires a bit of specialty shopping for chiles, this sauce is astounding. Look for ancho and pasilla chiles in the Mexican aisle of the grocery store or in plastic bags near the produce. Use this sauce not only on the Chicken Enchiladas with Salsa Verde and Smoked Ancho and Pasilla Sauce (page 184), but also to complement plain roasted chicken or grilled pork chops. It's also really wonderful on pulled pork instead of barbecue sauce.

1 pound dried ancho chiles

1 pound dried pasilla chiles

2 small yellow onions, coarsely chopped

6 Roma (plum) tomatoes, cored, coarsely chopped

6 garlic cloves

1 tablespoon rice vinegar

1 teaspoon sugar

1 teaspoon kosher salt

2 tablespoons neutral oil (such as canola or vegetable)

Preheat the broiler to high.

Turn a gas burner to high. Working with one dried chile at a time, use tongs to hold them just over the flames, rotating until puffed and fragrant, about 30 seconds. If you don't have a gas stove, you can roast the chiles under the broiler. Transfer the chiles to a work surface and let them cool. Stem and seed the chiles.

Place the onions, tomatoes, and garlic on a baking sheet or in an oven-safe skillet and broil, stirring them now and then, until charred all over, about 15 minutes. You really want some char on the vegetables.

Transfer the chiles and the charred vegetables to a medium pot and add the vinegar, sugar, and salt. Add 1 cup cold water and set the pot over high heat. Bring the mixture to a boil, lower the heat, and simmer until the vegetables are very soft, about 15 minutes.

Transfer the contents of the pot to a blender or food processor and puree until smooth. Strain the sauce through a fine-mesh sieve to make it extra smooth.

Rinse out the pot you cooked the vegetables in and wipe it dry. Place the oil in the pot and set it over medium-high heat. When the oil is hot, add the strained sauce to the pot and cook, stirring, until the sauce has thickened slightly and concentrated, about 4 minutes. Let the sauce cool to room temperature and then use immediately or store in a covered container in the refrigerator for up to 1 week.

Salsa Verde

Salsa verde, made with fresh tomatillos, can be served on its own with chips or as a taco topping or even as a sauce for scrambled eggs. We also use it on the Fried Green Tomato Salad with Salsa Verde and Queso Fresco (page 112).

1 pound tomatillos (about 10 medium), husked and washed well, cored, and coarsely chopped

1 small yellow onion, coarsely chopped

4 garlic cloves

1 jalapeño, seeded and coarsely chopped

Large handful of fresh cilantro (tender stems included), coarsely chopped

1 teaspoon kosher salt

Place the tomatillos, onion, garlic, and jalapeño in a large pot and add just enough cold water to cover. Bring the water to a boil and then reduce the heat to maintain a simmer. Cook until the vegetables are soft, about 15 minutes. Reserve $\frac{1}{2}$ cup of the cooking liquid and then drain the vegetables in a colander or sieve. Place the reserved cooking liquid and the vegetables in a blender with the cilantro and the salt. Blend until smooth. Serve immediately. Leftovers can be stored in an airtight container in the refrigerator for up to 1 week; bring to room temperature before serving.

Chicken Tinga

Makes about 3 cups

Not only is this stewed chicken wonderful (and essential!) in the Chicken Enchiladas with Salsa Verde and Smoked Ancho and Pasilla Sauce (page 184), it also works as a filling for quesadillas, tacos, or just served on its own with Island Rice Pilaf (page 256) and Fajita Black Beans (page 255). The chipotle peppers (canned smoked jalapeños) are easy to find with the Mexican ingredients in the grocery store.

1 small red onion, coarsely chopped

Large handful of fresh cilantro leaves, coarsely chopped

3 Roma (plum) tomatoes, cored, coarsely chopped

2 canned chipotle peppers in adobo sauce, plus 2 tablespoons adobo sauce from the can

2 tablespoons tomato paste

2 garlic cloves, minced

2 cups high-quality store-bought chicken stock

Kosher salt

2 tablespoons neutral oil (such as canola or vegetable)

1½ pounds boneless, skinless chicken thighs

Place the red onion, cilantro, tomatoes, chipotles and adobo sauce, tomato paste, garlic, stock, and ½ teaspoon salt in a food processor or blender and puree until smooth. Set aside.

Place the oil in a large pot set over high heat. Season the chicken thighs generously with salt and add them to the pot (work in batches as necessary). Cook, turning now and then, until browned on both sides, about 8 minutes. Add the pureed tomato mixture and bring the mixture to a boil. Reduce the heat to maintain a simmer and partially cover the pot. Simmer the chicken, giving the whole thing a stir now and then, until the chicken is incredibly tender, about 1 hour. Use two forks or tongs to shred the chicken directly in the pot. Serve hot.

Jerk Chicken

Jimmy brought this recipe back from Jamaica. Fun fact: The song "Jamaica Mistaica" was a result of one of his trips to Jamaica to learn the recipe. We like to serve this with Island Rice Pilaf (page 256) and Cilantro-Lime Coleslaw (page 242). It's especially terrific for a party because it's easy to make a large batch and it can be made ahead (just warm it up in a 300°F oven). If you'd like, you could also finish it on a charcoal grill instead of under the broiler for extra-smoky flavor.

1 small red onion, coarsely chopped

3 garlic cloves, minced

1 jalapeño, seeded and coarsely chopped

1 tablespoon fresh thyme leaves

3 tablespoons soy sauce

¼ cup high-quality store-bought chicken stock (or water)

2 tablespoons neutral oil (such as canola or vegetable)

½ teaspoon freshly ground black pepper

½ teaspoon ground cinnamon

1 teaspoon ground ginger

¼ teaspoon ground allspice

½ teaspoon kosher salt

2 chickens, quartered

Place the onion, garlic, jalapeño, thyme, soy sauce, stock, oil, pepper, cinnamon, ginger, allspice, and salt in a blender or food processor and puree until smooth.

Place the marinade in a large resealable plastic bag and add the chicken quarters. Seal the bag and rub the marinade all over the chicken. Refrigerate, turning the bag at least once, for at least 12 hours and up to 24 hours. Take the bag out of the fridge an hour before you're ready to cook.

Preheat the oven to 350°F.

Evenly space the chicken pieces in a large roasting pan or on a baking sheet (anything large enough to hold the chicken in a single layer), making sure they're skin-side up. If there's any extra marinade in the bag, pour it on top of the chicken.

Bake the chicken until the meat is tender and completely cooked through (a digital thermometer inserted into the thickest part of the thigh should register 165°F), about 1 hour 15 minutes.

Once the chicken is cooked through, turn your broiler to high and broil the chicken, skin side up, until charred in spots, about 5 minutes.

Transfer the chicken to a serving platter and spoon over some of the pan juices. Serve immediately.

Buttermilk Fried Chicken with Country Gravy

Serves 4

When we closed the deal on the Margaritaville on Broadway in Nashville, we knew our Gulf Coast Floridian menu needed a few nods to the "Third Coast." We committed to producing an awesome fried chicken and gravy that could hold its own in the land of "Meat Plus Three" plates. This Buttermilk Fried Chicken has been a top-selling entrée ever since. It's best if you let the chicken sit in the seasoned buttermilk in the fridge overnight, but a quick dip will be okay. The chicken can be kept warm on a wire rack in a 300°F oven for 30 minutes, if you want to make it ahead or are making a large batch.

2 slices bacon, finely diced

2 tablespoons plus 1 cup all-purpose flour

1 cup high-quality store-bought chicken stock

¼ cup heavy cream

Kosher salt

1 cup buttermilk

2 tablespoons Margaritaville House Spice Blend (page 128)

1 cup cornflakes, crushed

Four 6-ounce boneless, skinless chicken breasts

Neutral oil (such as canola or vegetable), for frying

Place the bacon in a heavy skillet set over medium heat. Cook, stirring, until the bacon is crisp and the fat has rendered, about 5 minutes. Use a slotted spoon to transfer the bacon to a paper towel–lined plate. Add 2 tablespoons of the flour to the bacon fat in the skillet. Cook, stirring continuously, until light golden brown (like a Golden Retriever), about 5 minutes. Slowly whisk in the stock and cream and cook, stirring now and then, until the mixture is thick enough to coat the back of a spoon. Stir in the crispy bacon and season the gravy with salt. Keep warm over very low heat.

Place the buttermilk and 1 tablespoon of the spice blend in a shallow baking dish and whisk together. Place the remaining 1 cup flour, the cornflakes, and remaining spice blend in another baking dish and whisk together.

Dip the chicken breasts in the buttermilk mixture and then lightly coat with the cornflake mixture. Do this one more time if you like extra-crunchy chicken.

Pour 1 inch of oil into a large heavy pot and heat the oil over medium heat. Test the oil: When a piece of chicken sizzles upon contact, it's ready. Carefully place the chicken breasts in the hot oil, working in batches as necessary so that they don't crowd the pot. Cook, turning the chicken pieces once while they cook, until golden brown all over and firm to the touch, about 10 minutes. Transfer the chicken to a paper towel–lined plate and fry the remaining chicken.

Serve hot, with the warm gravy alongside.

Shrimp Mofongo al Ajillo

Serves 4

Popular in Puerto Rico with origins in Africa, mofongo refers to mashed plantains that are often served with something with a fragrant sauce that the mofongo can absorb, not unlike shrimp and grits. Carlo created the most amazing sautéed shrimp to go with the mofongo, heavy on the garlic and tomato. These shrimp would be equally delicious tossed with a pound of cooked pasta or served on their own with some rice and diced avocado. Serve this dish when you want something hearty but unexpected.

3 large vine-ripened tomatoes

Kosher salt

1 pound medium shrimp, peeled and deveined (preferably Key West pink shrimp)

8 garlic cloves, minced

¼ cup minced fresh parsley

1 teaspoon pimentón (Spanish smoked sweet paprika)

½ teaspoon freshly ground black pepper

5 tablespoons olive oil

2 green plantains, peeled and cut into ¼-inch-thick rounds

Neutral oil (such as canola or vegetable)

3 tablespoons unsalted butter

½ cup dry white wine

¼ teaspoon red pepper flakes

Small handful of fresh parsley leaves, minced

Cut each tomato in half. Working over a large bowl, grate the cut side of each half on the coarse holes of a box grater. Discard the skins. Stir 1 teaspoon salt into the grated tomato pulp and set aside at room temperature.

Place the shrimp in a large bowl with half the garlic, the parsley, pimentón, black pepper, ½ teaspoon salt, and 2 tablespoons of the olive oil. Mix well to combine. Cover the bowl and refrigerate so the shrimp can marinate while you prepare the mofongo.

Pour 1 inch of neutral oil into a large pot and heat the oil over medium-high heat. Test the oil: When a piece of plantain sizzles upon contact, it's ready. Add the plantain slices to the hot oil,

(continued)

working in batches as necessary to avoid crowding, and fry, turning the pieces now and then, until golden brown all over, about 3 minutes. Transfer the plantains to a paper towel to drain and then transfer them to a large bowl with the remaining garlic and 1 tablespoon kosher salt. Crush with a potato masher until they're really well crushed (like lumpy mashed potatoes). Set the mofongo aside.

Take the shrimp out of the refrigerator. Place the remaining 3 tablespoons olive oil and the butter in a large nonstick skillet set over medium-high heat. Once the butter melts, add half the shrimp in an even layer and cook until they're browned on the bottom, about 1½ minutes. Turn each shrimp over and cook until browned on the second side, 1½ minutes more. Transfer the shrimp to a plate and repeat with the remaining shrimp. Once all the shrimp are cooked, return the first batch to the skillet and add the wine, red pepper flakes, and the reserved tomato pulp. Bring the mixture to a boil and then reduce the heat to low and cook, letting the mixture reduce, for about 5 minutes while you shape the mofongo.

Brush the inside of a small bowl with neutral oil (about 1 teaspoon) and place one-quarter of the mofongo in it. Press the mofongo in the bowl to create a domed shape and then invert it onto a dinner plate. Repeat the process three more times so that you end up with 4 portions of mofongo. Stir the parsley into the shrimp and then divide the shrimp and its sauce among the plates. Serve immediately.

Spear
Fishing
with Carlo

Outside-Optional Cajun Clambake

Serves 6

No digging holes for this clambake. It doesn't require shoveling in sand or gathering seaweed or anything at all labor-intensive. All you do is layer the ingredients in a large pot in order of how fast they cook, cover it, turn on the flame, and that's that! The andouille sausage, celery, and green bell pepper add a distinctly Cajun flavor to the seafood and corn. If you can get your hands on some crawfish, feel free to add them to the pot.

1 pound andouille sausage, cut into 1-inch pieces

1 large yellow onion, cut into ½-inch pieces

2 celery stalks, cut into ½-inch pieces

1 green bell pepper, cut into ½-inch pieces

2 fresh or dried bay leaves

3 garlic cloves, minced

4 ears corn, shucked, cut into 1-inch rounds

4 dozen littleneck clams, scrubbed

4 pounds mussels, scrubbed and debearded

2 pounds shell-on large shrimp

2 cups beer (preferably LandShark Lager)

Plenty of melted butter, for serving

Place the andouille in the bottom of a large pot and top with the onion, celery, bell pepper, and bay leaves. Sprinkle the garlic on top of the vegetables and then top with the corn, clams, mussels, and shrimp. Pour the beer over everything. Place the pot over high heat and cover tightly. Cook until steam is coming out from under the lid, about 15 minutes, then reduce the heat to medium-low and cook until the shrimp are bright pink and opaque throughout and the mussels and clams are open, 10 to 15 minutes more. Use large slotted spoons to transfer the contents of the pot to large serving platters or bowls. Fill little bowls with melted butter and give everyone their own so no one needs to worry about double-dipping.

Serve immediately, with a large empty bowl for discarding the shells and corncobs and plenty of napkins.

Sardinian Seafood Stew

Carlo would happily eat this every single day. Simple and full of the freshest seafood, this is just his kind of thing. Feel free to mix and match the seafood; just be sure to use whatever you love and whatever is the best quality you can find. Fregola, toasted Sardinian pasta that looks a lot like pearl couscous, is increasingly available in supermarkets and is sometimes available in seafood shops, and you can always find it online.

1½ cups fregola

3 large vine-ripened tomatoes, halved

Kosher salt

¼ cup olive oil, plus more for serving

8 garlic cloves, peeled and left whole

2 pounds cleaned calamari (squid), tentacles separated and bodies cut into thin rings

1 pound small clams (preferably Manila), cleaned

12 large shrimp, head on if possible

½ cup cognac

1 cup dry white wine

8 cups Lobster Stock (page 118) or high-quality store-bought seafood stock

1 pound mussels, scrubbed and debearded

4 tablespoons finely chopped fresh parsley leaves

1 tablespoon red pepper flakes

½ pound fresh fish (whatever is good!), cut into 2-inch pieces

Freshly ground black pepper

4 thick slices bread, toasted

Bring a small saucepan of water to a boil. Add the fregola and cook until just tender but not completely cooked through, about 10 minutes. Drain the fregola and set aside.

Working over a large bowl, grate the cut side of each tomato on the coarse holes of a box grater. Discard the skins. Stir 2 teaspoons of salt into the grated tomato pulp and set aside.

Place half of the olive oil and the garlic in a large pot set over medium heat. Cook, stirring, until the garlic is light golden brown, about 1 minute. Add the calamari and raise the heat to medium-high. Cook, stirring, until the calamari is light golden brown, about 2 minutes, then add the tomato pulp, clams, and shrimp. Cook, stirring, until most of the liquid has evaporated, about 2 minutes.

(continued)

Add the cognac, increase the heat to high, and let the mixture come to a boil. Cook for a minute to burn off the alcohol. Add the wine, stock, and mussels, and bring the mixture to a boil. Reduce the heat to medium and cook, stirring now and then, until all the clams and mussels are open (discard any that refuse to budge) and the shrimp are cooked through, about 8 minutes. Add 1 tablespoon of the parsley, the red pepper flakes, and the fregola and stir well to combine. Cook just until the fregola is completely tender, about 8 minutes.

Meanwhile, place the remaining olive oil in a small nonstick skillet set over medium-high heat. Season the fish on both sides with salt and pepper and cook the fish, turning it once, until lightly browned on both sides and firm to the touch, about 2 minutes per side.

Place one piece of toast in each of four shallow bowls and then evenly divide the fish and stew among the bowls. Top each one with some of the remaining parsley and drizzle about 1 tablespoon olive oil on each serving. Serve immediately.

Pan-Seared Halibut with Artichoke Ragout

Serves 4

One of the most popular entrées at JWB, this dish is also a lesson in how to cook a piece of simple fish beautifully. The light coating of bread crumbs adds lots of texture.

Four 8-ounce center-cut halibut fillets

4 teaspoons kosher salt

2 teaspoons freshly ground black pepper

1 cup fine bread crumbs

3 tablespoons grapeseed oil

4 tablespoons (½ stick) unsalted butter

1 lemon, thinly sliced

Artichoke Ragout (recipe follows)

3 tablespoons olive oil

Small handful of fresh parsley leaves, coarsely chopped

Preheat the oven to 400°F.

Use 1 teaspoon of the kosher salt and ½ teaspoon of the black pepper to season both sides of each piece of fish. Place the bread crumbs in a shallow bowl and dredge the fish on both sides with the bread crumbs, pressing them into the fish so that they adhere. Shake off any excess bread crumbs.

Place the grapeseed oil in a large oven-safe nonstick pan set over medium heat. Once it's nice and hot, add the fish in a single layer and scatter the lemon slices around the fish. Cook until the fish and lemon slices are lightly browned on each side, about 3 minutes per side. Place 1 tablespoon of the butter on each piece of fish and transfer the skillet to the oven. Roast until the fish is completely cooked through, about 3 minutes.

Add the Artichoke Ragout to the pan. Evenly drizzle the olive oil over the fish and sprinkle with the parsley. Serve immediately.

MAIN DISHES 203

Artichoke Ragout

Sautéed artichokes are so lovely underneath the halibut and can be a side dish for nearly anything. They pair especially well with roasted chicken and seared scallops. You can also stir them together with cooked pasta or into a risotto. The lemon water keeps the artichokes from browning and the little bit of flour in the soaking liquid helps to draw out some of the artichoke's natural bitterness (this is a tip Carlo learned in a Michelin-starred restaurant).

½ cup all-purpose flour

3 tablespoons fresh lemon juice

4 large artichokes

¼ cup olive oil

4 garlic cloves, minced

1 teaspoon coarse sugar (preferably turbinado) or granulated sugar

1 teaspoon kosher salt

2 tablespoons unsalted butter

¼ cup dry white wine

¼ cup high-quality store-bought vegetable or chicken stock (or water)

½ cup whole pitted Kalamata olives

Large handful of fresh parsley leaves, finely chopped

Place the flour and lemon juice in a large bowl with 1 cup cold water and whisk together to form a paste. Add 10 cups more water and whisk well to combine.

Remove the tough dark outer leaves from artichokes. Using a serrated knife, trim off and discard 1 inch from the top of each artichoke. Trim the stems and remove the tough outer layer with a vegetable peeler. Halve the artichokes lengthwise. Use a spoon to scrape out and discard the choke from the heart of each artichoke. Cut the prepared artichoke halves into ½-inch slices and place them in the bowl of flour-and-lemon water as you go.

Once you've prepared all the artichokes, drain them and pat them dry on a kitchen towel.

Place the oil in the largest skillet you have and set over medium-high heat. Add the garlic and cook until the garlic begins to sizzle, about 20 seconds. Add the artichokes in a single layer (do this in batches if necessary, depending on the size of your skillet—you want the artichokes to brown, not steam). Sprinkle the artichokes with the sugar and salt and cook, stirring now and then, until deeply browned all over, about 6 minutes. Add the butter, wine, and stock and raise the heat to high. Bring the mixture to a boil, reduce the heat to medium-low, and cover the skillet. Cook until the artichokes are very tender and the liquid has reduced, about 5 minutes. Stir in the olives and parsley and season the artichokes with salt. Serve immediately.

Seared Grouper with Fresh Mango Salsa

Serves 4

A simple mango salsa takes an ordinary piece of fish from so-so to so special. Like our Pineapple Salsa (page 156), it can also be served next to a bowl of tortilla chips with a pitcher of margaritas. The grouper could be swapped out for any kind of fish or even grilled shrimp or chicken.

1 cup finely diced fresh mango

½ cup finely diced cucumber

2 tablespoons minced fresh red onion

½ jalapeño, seeded and minced

½ fresh red chile pepper, seeded and minced

3 tablespoons fresh lime juice

Kosher salt

Freshly ground black pepper

Four 6-ounce pieces grouper or other firm white-fleshed fish, such as snapper or mahimahi

2 tablespoons neutral oil (such as canola or vegetable)

Small handful of fresh cilantro leaves

Preheat the oven to 400°F.

Place the mango, cucumber, onion, jalapeño, red chile, and lime juice in a bowl. Sprinkle with a large pinch of salt and stir together. Set aside.

Lightly season the fish all over with salt and pepper. Place the oil in a medium cast-iron skillet set over medium-high heat. Once it's nice and hot, add the fish and cook, turning the pieces once, until well browned on both sides, about 2 minutes per side. Transfer the skillet to the oven and cook the fish until it is firm to the touch and flakes easily when pushed with a fork or a paring knife, about 5 minutes.

Transfer the fish to a serving platter and spoon the mango salsa and cilantro leaves on top. Serve immediately.

Crispy Sicilian-Style Pounded Tuna Steaks

Serves 4

A very unexpected dish, these crispy tuna steaks are delicious. Treated almost like a chicken cutlet, the tuna gets pounded thin and coated with a delicious mustard and olive oil mixture that not only helps the bread crumbs adhere, but also keeps the tuna from drying out. Serve with a simple salad made of shaved fennel, grapefruit segments, and olives dressed with just olive oil and lemon juice.

¾ cup olive oil, plus more as needed

1 tablespoon Dijon mustard

¼ teaspoon honey

1 scallion, minced

1 teaspoon minced fresh thyme

2 teaspoons minced fresh ginger

¼ teaspoon kosher salt

¼ teaspoon freshly ground black pepper

1½ cups plain bread crumbs

1 pound fresh sushi-grade ahi tuna loin, in one whole piece

Place the olive oil, mustard, honey, scallion, thyme, ginger, salt, and pepper in a large baking dish and whisk well to combine. Place the bread crumbs in another baking dish.

Cut the tuna into ½-inch-thick slices. Brush two large pieces of parchment paper with a little olive oil (about 1 tablespoon each) and place a tuna slice on top of one. Place the second piece of parchment, oiled-side down, on top of the tuna. Use a meat pounder to delicately and evenly pound the tuna until it's ¼ inch thick. Repeat the process with the rest of the tuna, oiling the parchment as needed between pieces.

Place the pounded tuna steaks into the marinade and coat well on both sides. Dredge the coated tuna steaks, one at a time, in the bread crumbs and press lightly so they adhere on both sides.

Meanwhile, place 1 tablespoon olive oil in a large nonstick skillet set over high heat. When it's nice and hot, place one breaded tuna steak in the skillet and cook just until it's golden brown on the bottom, about 30 seconds. Carefully turn the tuna and cook just until the second side is light brown, about 30 seconds more. Transfer the tuna to a serving platter and repeat the process with the rest of the tuna, oiling the skillet as needed between pieces. Serve immediately.

Coho Salmon in Lemongrass-Miso Broth

Serves 4

For an elegant dinner at home, try this light, lovely salmon with the most fragrant broth. We love rich coho salmon from the Pacific Ocean, but use whatever type of salmon you love or any fresh fish. This also goes really well with cooked rice or another grain such as quinoa.

1 cup sake

1 cup white miso paste

½ cup mirin

Four 6-ounce skin-on coho salmon fillets

¾ pound fresh ginger

2 large fresh lemongrass stalks, halved

4 cups high-quality store-bought chicken stock

4 cups high-quality store-bought fish stock

¾ cup coarsely chopped fresh cilantro

¾ cup coarsely chopped fresh scallions

2 fresh red chiles, coarsely chopped

1 pound wild mushrooms, tough stems discarded, coarsely chopped

Kosher salt and freshly ground black pepper

3 tablespoons olive oil, plus more for serving

Large handful fresh pea tendrils (or minced chives)

Place the sake, ¼ cup of the miso paste, and the mirin in a small bowl and whisk together. Place the mixture in a large resealable bag and add the fish. Squeeze out all of the air and seal the bag. Refrigerate the salmon, turning the bag over at least once, for at least 1 hour and up to 12 hours.

Meanwhile, pound the ginger and lemongrass with the flat side of a large knife or a meat pounder to break up the fibers. Place the ginger and lemongrass in a large pot and add the remaining ¾ cup miso paste, the stocks, cilantro, and scallions. Set the pot over high heat and bring the stock to a boil. Reduce the heat to low and simmer for 20 minutes to really develop the flavors. Add the chiles and simmer for 5 minutes more to infuse the liquid with chile flavor.

Line a colander with cheesecloth and place it over a large bowl. Strain the broth through the colander and discard the solids. Wipe out the pot and return the broth to it. Place the mushrooms in the broth and keep it warm over low heat while you cook the salmon. Season the broth to taste with salt.

Remove the salmon from the marinade and pat the pieces dry with paper towels. Season the pieces all over with salt and pepper.

Place the oil in a large nonstick skillet set over medium-high heat. Place the salmon pieces skin-side down in the skillet, working in batches as necessary to prevent crowding, and cook until the skin is crispy, about 2 minutes. Carefully turn the pieces over and cook until the second side is browned, about 2 minutes more.

Place one piece of salmon, skin-side up, in each of four shallow serving bowls. Divide the broth and mushrooms evenly among the bowls. Drizzle each bowl with a little olive oil (about 2 teaspoons) and evenly sprinkle with the pea tendrils (or chives). Serve immediately.

Salt-Crusted Whole Snapper

Here's a showstopper. This fish makes for the most dramatic, beautiful presentation. It looks really impressive, as if it was very difficult to prepare, but it's actually quite simple. The salt keeps in the heat and steam and perfectly cooks the fish. You can use a whole striped sea bass or grouper instead of the snapper. Serve with grilled asparagus and roasted potatoes.

4 large egg whites

8 cups kosher salt

1 tablespoon minced fresh thyme, plus 1 whole sprig

1 tablespoon minced fresh rosemary, plus 1 whole sprig

1 tablespoon minced fresh marjoram (optional)

1 large whole snapper (about 3 pounds), guts and gills removed, but fine to leave scales on

2 garlic cloves, thinly sliced

2 lemons, thinly sliced

3 tablespoons high-quality extra-virgin olive oil

Preheat the oven to 400°F.

Place the egg whites and a pinch of salt in the bowl of a stand mixer fitted with the whisk attachment (or use a large bowl and a handheld mixer or a whisk and some elbow grease) and beat until they hold stiff peaks. Use a rubber spatula to slowly fold in the salt and minced herbs. You should be able to pack the mixture as if it were a snowball.

Place half the salt mixture on a baking sheet in an even layer about $\frac{1}{2}$ inch thick over an area slightly larger than the fish. Place the fish on top of the salt layer and stuff the body with the thyme and rosemary sprigs, the sliced garlic, and half the lemon slices. Cover the fish with the remaining salt mixture, packing it so the fish is totally enclosed, but leave a fish fin sticking out of the salt. This will be your indicator as to whether the fish is cooked through.

Roast the fish until the fin can be pulled out with no resistance, 15 to 20 minutes.

Present the fish at the table in its salt crust, since it looks amazing! Crack the crust and remove the chunks of salt from the fish. Carefully pull off and discard the skin on top of the fish. Use a fork and a spoon to lift the flesh off the bones and transfer it to a serving platter. Lift off and discard the bones and then transfer the flesh from the bottom side to the platter. Drizzle the fish with the olive oil and serve immediately, with the remaining lemon slices for squeezing over.

LandShark Beer–Battered Fish

Serves 4

When we came out with our beer, LandShark Lager (which was awarded Best Island-Style Lager by the North American Brewers Association, yay!), we celebrated by organizing a Sharktoberfest during the month of October. We challenged all our chefs across all our restaurants to come up with recipes that used LandShark. There were all sorts of creative items, including a beer barbecue sauce, but this simple beer-battered fish is the item that's stood the test of time and is the beer recipe we use to this day. Serve with Oven Fries (page 254) for the full fish-and-chips experience at home.

1 large egg

1 cup LandShark Lager

1 teaspoon baking powder

1 teaspoon garlic powder

Pinch of kosher salt, plus more as needed

Pinch of freshly ground black pepper

Pinch of cayenne pepper

1 cup all-purpose flour

Neutral oil (such as canola or vegetable), for frying

1½ pounds cod (or other firm white fish such as grouper), cut into thick strips

Malt vinegar, for serving

Place the egg in a large bowl and whisk it well. Whisk in the beer, baking powder, garlic powder, salt, black pepper, and cayenne. Whisk in the flour.

Pour 1 inch of oil into a large heavy pot and heat the oil over medium heat. Test the oil: When a pinch of batter sizzles upon contact, it's ready. Carefully dip the fish into the batter just to lightly coat it and then place the pieces in the hot oil. Work in batches as necessary so the fish doesn't crowd the pot. Cook, turning the fish pieces a few times while they cook, until golden brown all over, about 4 minutes. Transfer the fish to a paper towel–lined plate and fry the rest (the fried fish can be kept warm on a wire rack in a 300°F oven while you fry the rest).

Sprinkle the hot fish with salt and serve immediately, with malt vinegar alongside.

Seafood Mac and Cheese

Serves 4 to 6

With equal parts fresh seafood and a rich, creamy sauce filled with Asiago and Boursin, this is not your ordinary mac and cheese. If you'd like to make this extra luxurious, you could substitute chopped lobster tails for some or all of the shrimp and crab.

FOR THE CHEESE SAUCE

1½ cups heavy cream

½ cup whole milk

2 teaspoons kosher salt

½ teaspoon garlic powder

¼ cup coarsely grated Asiago cheese

Pinch of cayenne pepper, or a few dashes of hot sauce

1 tablespoon cornstarch

One 5.2-ounce package Boursin cheese (plain or whatever flavor you like)

FOR THE PASTA

½ cup panko bread crumbs

Kosher salt

1 pound short, ridged pasta (preferably cavatappi)

3 tablespoons olive oil

2 garlic cloves, minced

1 pound small shrimp, peeled and deveined

½ pound fresh or pasteurized jumbo lump crabmeat

Small handful of fresh chives, minced

MAKE THE CHEESE SAUCE: Place the cream, milk, salt, garlic powder, Asiago, and cayenne in a small saucepan set over high heat. Cook the mixture, stirring, until it comes to a boil and then immediately reduce the heat to low. Meanwhile, place the cornstarch in a small bowl with 3 tablespoons water and whisk together. Whisk the cornstarch mixture into the simmering sauce and cook until thickened, about 1 minute. Crumble the Boursin into the sauce and whisk until smooth. Keep the sauce warm over low heat.

MAKE THE PASTA: Place the panko in a large skillet set over medium heat. Cook, stirring, until golden brown, about 5 minutes. Transfer the panko to a bowl and set aside.

Meanwhile, bring a large pot of water to a boil and salt it generously. Add the pasta and cook for 2 minutes less than directed on the package to make sure it doesn't end up overcooked. Use a teacup to reserve about 1 cup of the pasta cooking water and drain the pasta in a colander.

Meanwhile, place the olive oil in the skillet you used for the panko and set it over medium-high heat. Add the garlic and shrimp and sprinkle with a large pinch of salt. Cook, turning the shrimp once as they cook, until bright pink and firm to the touch, about 4 minutes.

Return the cooked pasta to the pot you cooked it in and add the shrimp, crabmeat, and warm cheese sauce. Give everything a good stir to combine. If the pasta seems a bit dry, add some of the reserved pasta cooking water to loosen it. Season the pasta with salt and transfer to a large serving bowl or to individual serving bowls.

Sprinkle the pasta with the toasted panko and chives and serve immediately.

Lobster Pasta

Carlo is half Italian and we especially appreciate his heritage when it comes to his pastas. This has become one of the most popular dishes at JWB and is one of the best ways to use his amazing Lobster Stock (page 118). If you can't find garganelli, orecchiette or penne are both good choices. Serve this for a simple yet elegant dinner party.

Kosher salt

1 pound garganelli pasta (or any short, ridged pasta)

4 tablespoons (½ stick) unsalted butter

½ pound broccoli rabe, coarsely chopped

1½ cups Lobster Stock (page 118)

1 pound raw Maine lobster meat, coarsely chopped

½ pound mixed wild mushrooms, tough stems discarded, coarsely chopped

2 tablespoons minced fresh parsley

1½ tablespoons fine bread crumbs, lightly toasted

Bring a large pot of water to a boil and salt it generously. Add the pasta and cook for 2 minutes less than directed on the package (it will finish cooking in the sauce). Use a teacup to reserve about 1 cup of the pasta cooking water and then drain the pasta in a colander.

Meanwhile, place the butter in a large skillet set over medium heat. Once it melts, add the broccoli rabe and a large pinch of salt and cook, stirring, until it's bright green, about 1 minute. Add the stock, lobster meat, and mushrooms and bring to a boil. Reduce the heat to maintain a simmer and cook until the lobster is just cooked through, about 3 minutes. Add the drained pasta to the skillet (if your skillet is not large enough, place the pasta and the contents of the skillet in the empty pot you cooked the pasta in and set it over medium heat). Cook, stirring, until the pasta absorbs all the sauce. If it's dry at all, just add a splash of the reserved cooking water. Season the pasta with salt and stir in the parsley.

Transfer the pasta to individual serving bowls and top each portion with some of the bread crumbs. Serve immediately.

Paella del Mar

When Carlo first started working in Florida, he worked with a chef who had worked with some of the best chefs in Spain. In fact, the chef had once spent time cooking in the Spanish king's brigade. Carlo learned how to make this paella from him. You don't always see aioli on paella, but the chef Carlo worked with was from Barcelona, where aioli gets put on so many things. Be sure to seek out Bomba or Calasparra rice (the types of rice traditionally used in paella, both available from tienda.com) for this. Carlo says that in a pinch, Uncle Ben's will do! If you're not in the mood for rice, this entire recipe can be made into *fideuà*, the Catalan dish of toasted pasta that's cooked with broth. Simply substitute *fideus* (sometimes called *fideos*, short pieces of Spanish pasta that can sourced on tienda.com as well) for the rice.

4 ½ cups Lobster Stock (page 118) or high-quality store-bought seafood stock, or 2 cups clam juice and 2 cups water

1 large yellow onion, coarsely chopped

1 red bell pepper, coarsely chopped

½ small green bell pepper, coarsely chopped

2 garlic cloves, minced

3 tablespoons olive oil

1 tablespoon tomato paste

1 tablespoon pimentón (Spanish smoked sweet paprika)

1 teaspoon kosher salt

½ teaspoon freshly ground black pepper

2 small Roma (plum) tomatoes, cored, seeded, and finely chopped

1 ¾ cups short-grain white rice (preferably Bomba or Calasparra)

12 littleneck clams, cleaned

½ pound cleaned calamari (squid), tentacles separated and bodies cut into thin rings

18 medium shell-on shrimp

1 pound high-quality firm white-fleshed fish (such as grouper, snapper, cobia, golden tile, or monkfish), cut into 2-inch pieces

1 pound mussels, scrubbed and debearded

Large handful of fresh parsley leaves, finely chopped

½ cup Lemon Aioli (page 58)

1 lemon, cut into wedges, for serving

Preheat the oven to 400°F.

Place the stock in a medium pot set over high heat. Bring it to a boil, reduce the heat to low, and keep it warm.

Place the onion, bell peppers, and garlic in a food processor and pulse until very finely chopped.

(continued)

Place the olive oil in a 13-inch paella pan (or the largest skillet you have, at least 12 inches in diameter) set over medium heat. Once it's nice and hot, add the onion mixture. Cook, stirring, until the vegetables are softened, about 10 minutes. Add the tomato paste, pimentón, salt, and black pepper. Cook, stirring continuously, until the mixture is really rich and has reduced, about 10 minutes. Add ½ cup of the hot stock, cover the pan, reduce the heat to medium-low, and simmer for 10 minutes. Uncover the pan and add the chopped tomatoes. Cook, uncovered, stirring now and then, until the liquid has nearly evaporated, about 10 minutes.

Add the rice to the pan and stir well to combine. Use your spoon to spread the rice and vegetables into a nice even layer. Pour the remaining 4 cups hot stock over the rice and raise the heat to high. Once the stock comes to a boil, reduce the heat to low and cook, uncovered, until the rice starts to get tender, about 8 minutes. Place the clams and calamari on top of the rice in an even layer and cook for 3 minutes. Add the shrimp and the fish in an even layer and place the pan in the oven. Roast for 5 minutes. Remove from the oven and evenly arrange the mussels on top. Return the paella to the oven and cook until the liquid has been absorbed, the rice is tender, the clams and mussels are open (discard any that refuse to budge), the calamari and shrimp are opaque and firm, and the fish flakes easily with a fork or a paring knife, about 10 minutes.

Let the paella sit at room temperature for 5 minutes. Sprinkle with the parsley and drizzle with the aioli. Serve immediately, with lemon wedges for squeezing over.

Jimmy's Jammin' Jambalaya

The first chef at our New Orleans restaurant put so much cayenne in the jambalaya that no one but him could eat it. Jimmy came by several times and never got past the first forkful. "Too spicy . . . tone it down . . ." he'd say. He explained that everyone wants to be able to take a bite and say to the table, "That's not too spicy. I can handle that. Give me the Tabasco, I want to make it spicier." He told the chef that by making the jambalaya so spicy to begin with, he was depriving the diner of that satisfaction. After that, the chef backed off the cayenne and the dish became a winner. You can make the chicken, sausage, and tomato base for the jambalaya ahead of time and then warm it just before adding the shrimp and rice.

4 tablespoons neutral oil (such as canola or vegetable)

½ pound andouille sausage, casings removed, crumbled

½ pound smoked pork sausage (such as kielbasa), halved lengthwise and thinly sliced into half-moons

¾ pound boneless, skinless chicken thighs, cut into bite-size cubes

1 small yellow onion, finely diced

2 celery stalks, finely diced

1 green bell pepper, finely diced

2 garlic cloves, minced

½ teaspoon dried thyme

½ teaspoon dried oregano

½ teaspoon freshly ground black pepper

Pinch of cayenne pepper

1 teaspoon kosher salt, plus more if needed

¼ cup all-purpose flour

1½ cups high-quality store-bought chicken stock

One 14.5-ounce can diced tomatoes, undrained

One 10-ounce can Ro*Tel Original diced tomatoes and green chiles

2 tablespoons Worcestershire sauce

1 pound medium shrimp, peeled and deveined

6 cups cooked white rice, warm

Place 2 tablespoons of the oil in a large heavy pot set over medium-high heat. Add the andouille, pork sausage, and chicken and cook, stirring now and then, until everything is browned and the chicken is firm to the touch, about 15 minutes.

Add the onion, celery, bell pepper, garlic, thyme, oregano, black pepper, cayenne pepper, and salt and stir well to combine. Cook, stirring now and then, until the vegetables are softened, about 10 minutes.

(continued)

Add the flour and stir well to combine. Cook until the flour gets ever so slightly browned, about 3 minutes. While stirring, slowly add the stock to form a smooth sauce. Add the tomatoes, Ro*Tel, and Worcestershire. Give everything a good stir and be sure to scrape the bottom to make sure you mix in any pieces of flavor that are stuck to the pot. Bring the mixture to a boil, reduce the heat to maintain a simmer, and cook for 20 minutes. Season the jambalaya with salt. At this point, the jambalaya can be cooled and stored in a covered container in the refrigerator for up to 1 week.

To serve, place the remaining 2 tablespoons oil in a large nonstick skillet set over high heat. Add the shrimp in an even layer, working in batches if needed, depending on the size of your pan, and cook until browned on both sides and just barely firm to the touch, about 5 minutes.

Fold the shrimp and cooked rice into the jambalaya and stir well to combine. Serve immediately.

Baby Back Ribs with Guava Barbecue Sauce

Serves 4

Made for a party, you can cook these ribs and make the sauce ahead of time. Cover and refrigerate them separately, and then when your friends come around, just warm them up and glaze them under the high heat of your broiler or on the grill. Serve with a platter of simple vegetables (like blanched asparagus and sliced radishes) and/or a big bowl of Cilantro-Lime Coleslaw (page 242) and a pile of Grilled Corn with Lime Butter (page 263). Guava paste usually comes in a round tin and is readily available in the international aisle of the grocery store (we like Goya brand).

1 tablespoon kosher salt

1 tablespoon garlic powder

2 teaspoons freshly ground black pepper

¼ cup fresh lime juice

4 pounds baby back rib racks, membranes removed

½ cup ketchup

1 cup guava paste

¼ cup fresh orange juice

1 tablespoon Worcestershire sauce

1 tablespoon dried red chile powder

1 teaspoon ground cumin

1 teaspoon dried thyme

¼ teaspoon ground allspice

Preheat the oven to 350°F.

Place the salt, garlic powder, pepper, and lime juice in a small bowl and stir together. Rub the mixture all over the ribs and place them on a baking sheet in an even layer. Pour 1 cup water around the ribs and cover the pan tightly with aluminum foil.

Bake the ribs until the meat is very tender, about 2 hours. Carefully remove the ribs from the oven and unwrap them. Pour off the cooking liquid but leave the ribs on the baking sheet.

While the ribs are baking, place the ketchup, guava paste, orange juice, Worcestershire, chile powder, cumin, thyme, and allspice in a small saucepan set over high heat. Bring to a boil, whisking to dissolve the guava paste and combine all the ingredients. Once it boils, turn off the heat and set the sauce aside.

Once the ribs are cooked and the sauce is done, either turn your broiler to high, preheat an outdoor grill to medium, or set a grill pan over medium heat. Grill or broil the ribs, basting with the guava barbecue sauce and turning them as they cook, until hot and glazed and charred in spots, about 8 minutes. Transfer the racks to a cutting board and cut into individual ribs, then transfer them to a serving platter.

Drizzle with any remaining guava barbecue sauce and serve warm, with a large roll of paper towels handy.

Pizza à la Minute

Serves 4

Call it pizza, call it flatbread, call it whatever you want. This is the easiest, most practical dough and requires no yeast, rising, or waiting whatsoever. Carlo learned to make it when he lived on Los Roques Island, where he had to make his own electricity with water from the ocean (that's a whole other recipe!) and worked with very limited ingredients. To make pizza in the restaurant where he worked, they just mixed flour with their homemade yogurt, and that was that. The recipe here is for classic tomato and mozzarella, but feel free to use any toppings you like. A favorite of ours is simple tomato sauce topped with cooked Italian sausage, cooked broccoli rabe, and mozzarella cheese. Or top this tomato-and-mozzarella pie with raw arugula and thinly sliced prosciutto after it comes out of the oven.

3½ cups "00" flour (Italian flour made for pizza and pasta)
or all-purpose flour, sifted, plus more for dusting

2 cups plain yogurt

1 tablespoon olive oil

1½ teaspoons kosher salt

2 cups your favorite tomato sauce

1 pound fresh mozzarella cheese, torn into bite-size pieces

Large handful of fresh basil leaves

Place the flour, yogurt, olive oil, and salt in a large bowl and mix with a wooden spoon. Once most of the yogurt has been absorbed, switch over to kneading with your hands. The dough will be sticky. Transfer the dough to a floured work surface and knead it until it feels smooth and no longer sticks to your hands, about 5 minutes (add as much flour as you need to make the dough nice and soft; it will probably take another cup all together). At this point, you can use the dough immediately or wrap it in plastic and keep it in the refrigerator for up to 2 days (bring it to room temperature before proceeding).

Preheat the oven to 450°F. Place a pizza stone on the bottom to heat up.

Divide the dough into quarters and use your hands to shape each piece into a small round and press it into a flat disc. Use a floured wooden rolling pin to shape each disc into a thin round. If the dough resists when you roll it, just let it rest for a few minutes and then continue. Transfer one piece of the dough to a pizza peel and quickly top it with $\frac{1}{2}$ cup of the tomato sauce and one-quarter of the cheese. Slide the pizza onto the stone and bake until the dough is golden brown and the toppings bubble, about 8 minutes. Sprinkle with some of the basil and cut into wedges.

Serve the first pizza immediately while you repeat the process with your remaining dough, sauce, cheese, and basil.

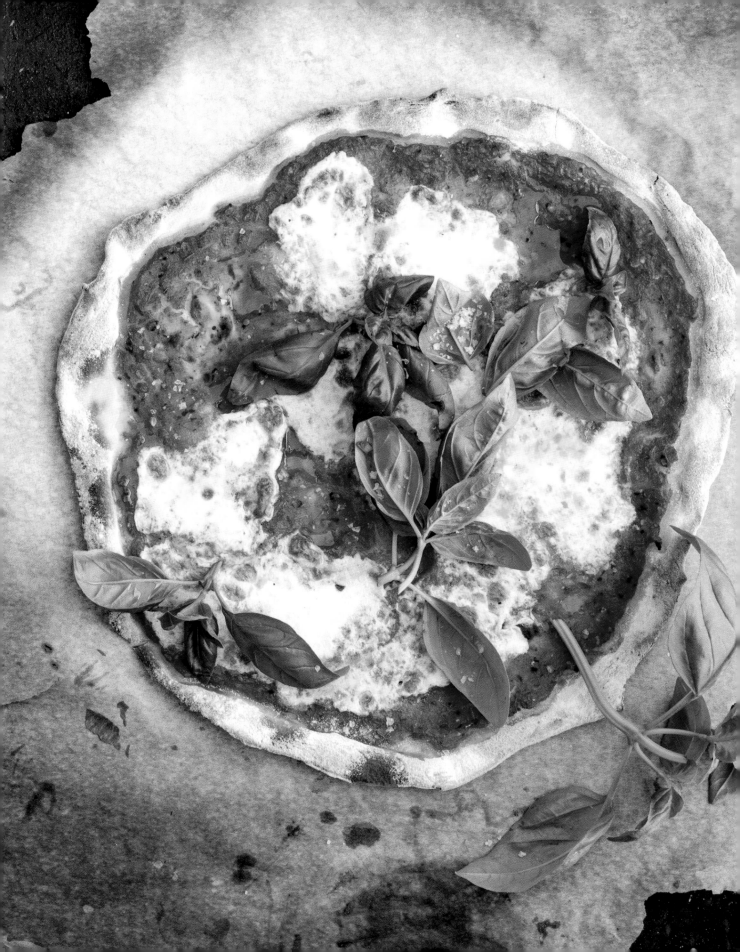

Side
Dishes

"THE SAUCE BOSS DOES HIS COOKIN' ON THE STAGE, STIRRIN' AND A-SINGIN' FOR HIS NIGHTLY WAGE. . . ."

You know that thing people say about how you're only as good as the company you keep? We feel that way about what goes on our plates. The main events are just as important as what comes with them. Side dishes can change the feeling of an entire meal. Be transported to a Mexican seaside town with a bowl of fresh Pico de Gallo (page 238) or visit the American South with a batch of Skillet Cornbread with Honey Butter (page 260). Even the simplest things like a piece of grilled fish or a store-bought rotisserie chicken can turn into the most memorable meals if they're served with something as special (and decadent) as JWB Creamed Spinach (page 253). Sometimes side dishes can even be the main event, such as the Pickled Jalapeño Mac and Cheese (page 264). From rich Yukon Gold Loaded Mashed Potatoes (page 245) to crunchy Cilantro-Lime Coleslaw (page 242), we've got a supporting player for every star in this chapter.

Pico de Gallo

Homemade pico de gallo, or fresh tomato salsa, is an essential part of our Volcano Nachos (page 36). We also like it on its own with good tortilla chips and a frosty margarita or an ice-cold LandShark Lager. Try serving it on top of eggs, on grilled fish or chicken, or in your favorite tacos.

1½ cups finely diced fresh tomatoes

1 small yellow onion, finely diced

Large handful of fresh cilantro leaves, finely chopped

1 jalapeño, seeded and minced

2 tablespoons fresh lime juice, plus more if needed

½ teaspoon kosher salt, plus more if needed

Place all the ingredients together in a large bowl and gently stir together. Taste for seasoning, adding more lime and/or salt as needed. Serve immediately.

Guacamole

Who doesn't love fresh, homemade guacamole? We find the most buttery avocados and gently mash them with all the works (red onion, juicy tomatoes, fresh cilantro, and bright lime juice). We like ours with fresh jalapeño, but feel free to leave it out if you prefer things mild. Our biggest piece of advice is to make it just before you eat it, just like we do at all our restaurants.

2 tablespoons minced red onion

1 garlic clove, minced

1 teaspoon kosher salt, plus more as needed

3 ripe Hass avocadoes, pitted, peeled, and coarsely chopped

1 tablespoon minced fresh cilantro leaves

1 tablespoon diced fresh tomato

1 jalapeño, minced (seeded if you like it not too spicy)

3 tablespoons fresh lime juice

Place the onion, garlic, and salt in a large mortar and pestle and grind them into a coarse paste. Add the avocado and smash it into the paste with a wooden spoon. Stir in the cilantro, tomato, jalapeño, and lime juice. Season the guacamole with salt and serve immediately.

Cilantro-Lime Coleslaw

Makes about 6 cups

While some coleslaw is like mayonnaise with a bit of cabbage, ours is just barely dressed, super crunchy, and fresh. We like it not only next to so many things (like the Jerk Chicken on page 190 and the Baby Back Ribs with Guava Barbecue Sauce on page 228), but also love it *on* so many things, including our Blackened Fish Sandwiches (page 152). Go ahead and make a double batch and keep it in the refrigerator. Your future self will be so happy.

¼ cup mayonnaise

¼ cup fresh lime juice

2 teaspoons sugar

1 tablespoon prepared horseradish

½ teaspoon kosher salt

4 cups very thinly sliced green cabbage

2 cups very thinly sliced red cabbage

1 carrot, coarsely grated

2 large handfuls of fresh cilantro leaves, finely chopped

Place the mayonnaise, lime juice, sugar, horseradish, and salt in a large bowl and whisk together. Add the cabbages, carrot, and cilantro and stir well to combine. Serve immediately or cover and refrigerate for up to 3 days.

Crispy Brussels Sprouts

While we fry these at the restaurant, a very hot oven crisps them just as well at home, and you don't have to worry about navigating a big pot of oil (plus, they're healthier). The pungent fish sauce mixed with bright lemon juice and salty Parmesan cheese makes the sprouts addictive. If you like, you could top these with some cooked, crumbled bacon (six slices should do) or crispy cubes of pancetta.

1½ pounds Brussels sprouts, bottoms trimmed, halved

3 tablespoons plus ¼ cup olive oil

½ teaspoon kosher salt

2 tablespoons fresh lemon juice

2 teaspoons fish sauce

Pinch of red pepper flakes

¼ cup shaved Parmesan cheese

½ teaspoon flaky salt (preferably Maldon)

2 tablespoons pickled mustard seeds (page 88, optional)

Preheat the oven to 450°F.

Place the Brussels sprouts on a baking sheet. Drizzle with 3 tablespoons of the olive oil and sprinkle with the kosher salt. Use your hands to mix everything well. Roast the sprouts, stirring them a few times while they cook, until they're dark brown and crispy at the edges, about 20 minutes.

Meanwhile, place the remaining ¼ cup olive oil in a large bowl and add the lemon juice, fish sauce, and red pepper flakes. Whisk well to combine.

Transfer the crispy sprouts to the dressing and add the Parmesan, flaky salt, and pickled mustard seeds, if using. Toss well to combine and then transfer to a serving platter. Serve immediately.

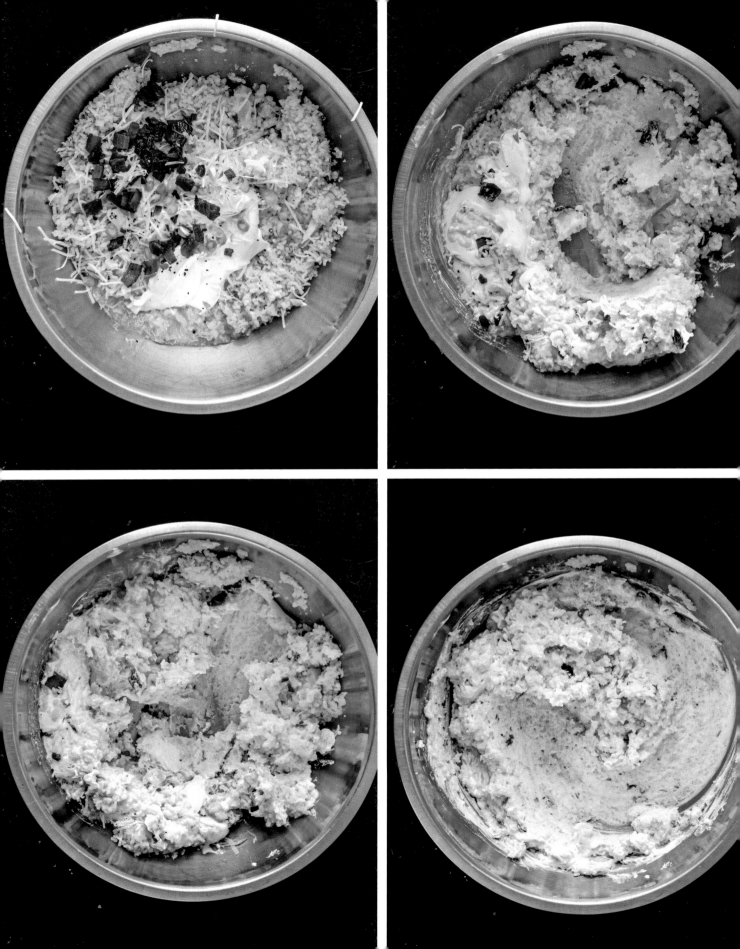

Yukon Gold Loaded Mashed Potatoes

Serves 4

With all of the memorable flavors of loaded potato skins, this mash is so comforting. If you want to make this ahead, just place the mashed potatoes in a baking dish and warm them up in a 300°F oven until they're piping hot (about 20 minutes) and then run them under the hot broiler to brown the top, if you'd like.

Kosher salt

2 pounds Yukon Gold potatoes, peeled and coarsely chopped

2 tablespoons unsalted butter, cubed

½ cup half-and-half

¼ cup coarsely grated Monterey Jack cheese

¼ cup coarsely grated sharp cheddar cheese

½ cup sour cream

6 slices bacon, cooked until crisp and crumbled

3 scallions, thinly sliced

Bring a large pot of water to a boil and salt it generously. Add the potatoes and cook until they're very tender, about 15 minutes. Drain the potatoes and push them through a ricer into a large bowl (or just place them in a large bowl and crush with a potato masher). Add the butter, half-and-half, both of the cheeses, sour cream, bacon, and scallions and mix well to combine. Season the potatoes with salt (about 1½ teaspoons). Serve immediately.

Spicy Red Onion Rings

Instead of using yellow onions and a bland batter for our onion rings, we use red onions and a buttermilk–hot sauce marinade. Try serving with any of our sauces like our Lemon Aioli (page 58) or our Mustard Sauce (page 42).

1 cup buttermilk

1 cup hot sauce (preferably Frank's RedHot or Crystal)

1½ cups all-purpose flour

½ cup cornstarch

2 teaspoons kosher salt, plus more for sprinkling

2 large red onions, cut into thick rounds, rings separated

Neutral oil (such as canola or vegetable), for frying

Place the buttermilk and hot sauce in a shallow baking dish and whisk together. Place the flour, cornstarch, and salt in another baking dish and whisk together.

Working with a few onion rings at a time, dip them in the buttermilk mixture and then lightly coat with the flour mixture. Do this one more time if you like extra-crunchy onion rings. Place the coated onion rings on a wire rack.

Pour 1 inch of neutral oil into a large heavy pot and heat the oil over medium heat. Test the oil: When a small onion ring sizzles upon contact, it's ready. Carefully place the onion rings into the hot oil, working in batches as necessary so they don't crowd the pot. Cook, turning the onion rings a few times while they cook, until golden brown all over, about 4 minutes. Transfer the onion rings to a paper towel–lined plate and continue frying the rest (the fried onion rings can be kept warm on a wire rack in a 300°F oven while you continue to fry the rest).

Serve the onion rings hot, sprinkled with extra salt.

Livin' Floridays

Lobster Hash Browns with Jalapeño Cheese

Serves 4

When regular hash browns just won't cut it, try these. Serve with grilled steak for a fancy dinner in the dining room or top these with poached eggs for a luxurious, hearty brunch outside on the deck. It's important not to skip the first step of the recipe. Clarifying the butter helps give the hash browns their unmistakable buttery flavor.

6 tablespoons (¾ stick) unsalted butter

1 medium yellow onion, thinly sliced

2 pounds russet potatoes, peeled and coarsely grated

1 tablespoon kosher salt

1 teaspoon freshly ground black pepper

1½ teaspoons cayenne pepper

¼ pound raw Maine lobster meat, coarsely chopped

¾ cup coarsely grated jalapeño cheddar cheese or pepper Jack cheese

Line a strainer with a coffee filter or a piece of cheesecloth and set it over a bowl.

Place the butter in a small pot set over high heat. Once it melts, let the butter cook until the white milk proteins float to the surface, about 3 minutes. Once the butter boils, reduce the heat to medium and cook until the white milk proteins sink to the bottom of the pot. Strain the butter through the coffee filter or cheesecloth and discard the solids.

Pour one-third of the clarified butter into an 8-inch nonstick skillet set over medium-high heat. Add the onion and cook, stirring now and then, until it's softened and dark golden brown, about 20 minutes.

Meanwhile, place the potatoes in the center of a kitchen towel and gather the ends to make a tight bundle. Squeeze the potatoes to remove all their excess water. Place the dried potatoes in a large bowl and add the salt, black pepper, and cayenne. Add the cooked onion (set the pan aside—no need to wash it) and mix the potato mixture well to combine.

Pour one-third of the clarified butter into the skillet you used for the onion and set it over medium heat. Add half the potato mixture and press it into an even layer. Top with the lobster meat and the cheese and then top with the remaining potatoes. Cook, pressing down with a spatula, until the bottom of the potatoes are golden brown, about 5 minutes. Place a plate that's larger in diameter than the skillet over the skillet and with one hand on the plate and one on the skillet's handle, quickly and carefully invert the hash browns onto the plate.

Place the remaining clarified butter in the skillet and slip the hash browns back into the pan, with the cooked side up. Cook, pressing down on the hash browns, until the bottom is golden brown, about 5 minutes. At this point, the potatoes and lobster should be cooked through and the cheese should be melted. Serve immediately.

JWB Creamed Spinach

Creamed spinach can be a yardstick for steakhouses, so we knew we had to nail the one we serve at JWB. Our version is heavy on both the spinach and the cream, and our custom steak seasoning and a generous pour of Worcestershire give it tons of flavor. You can assemble the dish up until the point of broiling, let it cool, and keep it covered in the refrigerator for up to a few days. When it's time to eat, just warm the spinach up in a 300°F oven (it will take about 20 minutes) and then run it under the hot broiler to brown the Parmesan on top.

4 tablespoons (½ stick) unsalted butter

1 small yellow onion, finely diced

3 tablespoons all-purpose flour

1½ teaspoons kosher salt

½ teaspoon freshly ground black pepper

1 cup whole milk

1 cup heavy cream

Three 10-ounce boxes frozen spinach, thawed, squeezed dry, and finely chopped

1 tablespoon JWB Steak Seasoning (page 171), or 1 teaspoon kosher salt plus ½ teaspoon freshly ground black pepper

3 tablespoons cream cheese

1 tablespoon Worcestershire sauce

¼ cup shaved Parmesan cheese

Preheat the broiler to high. Position an oven rack so it's 6 inches away from the heating element.

Place the butter in a medium saucepan set over medium heat. Once it melts, add the onion and cook, stirring now and then, until softened but not browned, about 8 minutes. Add the flour, salt, and pepper. Cook, stirring, for a minute just to cook off some of the raw flour taste. Slowly stir in the milk and cream, scraping the bottom and sides of the saucepan as you add the liquids to loosen all the flour. Cook until the mixture is slightly thickened, about 2 minutes. Add the spinach, JWB Steak Seasoning, cream cheese, and Worcestershire sauce. Cook until the spinach is bubbling, about 5 minutes. Transfer the creamed spinach to a baking dish and sprinkle with the Parmesan. Broil the spinach until the cheese is melted and bubbling, about 2 minutes. Serve hot.

Oven Fries

As vendors of much bar food, sandwiches, and burgers, we have served many a French fry. If we're being honest though, we never make French fries at home since they can be really messy and time-consuming to prepare. Enter these oven fries. They are way easier to make at home than traditional French fries, and a lot healthier, too. The trick is to blanch them first to get the inside of the potatoes soft, then roast them on a preheated baking sheet with plenty of olive oil to crisp them. Serves these with burgers, sandwiches, and especially with LandShark Beer–Battered Fish (page 217). Don't forget something to dip them in, whether it's just ketchup or mayonnaise, or any of our sauces like Calypso Sauce (page 50) or Paradise Island Sauce (page 129).

4 medium Yukon Gold potatoes, peeled, if you'd like,
and cut into ½-inch-thick fries

3 tablespoons olive oil

Kosher salt

Preheat the oven to 450°F. Place a baking sheet in the oven to heat up.

Place the potatoes in a large pot and add cold water to cover by 1 inch. Set the heat to high and cover the pot. When the water just comes to a boil, turn off the heat and drain the potatoes well (they won't be cooked through all the way). Place the potatoes on a kitchen towel to dry completely.

Take the hot baking sheet out of oven and drizzle with 2 tablespoons of the olive oil. Place the potatoes on the pan in a single layer and drizzle with the remaining 1 tablespoon olive oil. Sprinkle generously with salt. Roast the potatoes, tossing them now and then, until golden brown all over, about 35 minutes. Season the fries with more salt and serve hot.

Fajita Black Beans

Serves 4 to 6 (makes about 4 cups)

A workhorse, these are our all-purpose black beans. With some rice, they're a healthy and complete meal (top with grated cheese, diced avocado, and a spoonful of Pico de Gallo, page 238). We also use these in many other dishes like Huevos Rancheros (page 16). Stretch these out with some vegetable or chicken stock, and you'll have black bean soup.

2 tablespoons neutral oil (such as canola or vegetable)

1 small red onion, finely diced

3 garlic cloves, minced

1 teaspoon ground cumin

1 teaspoon dried red chile powder

2 teaspoons kosher salt

Two 15-ounce can black beans, undrained

Place the oil in a medium saucepan set over medium-high heat. Add the onion and cook, stirring now and then, until softened and the edges are a little bit browned, about 10 minutes. Add the garlic, cumin, chile powder, and salt and cook, stirring, until very fragrant, about 2 minutes. Add the black beans and their liquid and bring the mixture to a boil. Reduce the heat so the beans are just at a simmer and cook, stirring now and then, until the flavors are well combined, about 15 minutes. Serve warm.

SIDE DISHES   255

Island Rice Pilaf

Full of color and flavor thanks to sautéed onions and peppers and coconut milk, this rice pilaf tastes as good as it looks. If you want to make it ahead of time, spread the cooked pilaf on a baking sheet or in a baking dish. Let it cool, cover, and refrigerate for up to 2 days. To serve, uncover it and warm it in a 300°F oven until heated through, about 15 minutes.

2 tablespoons olive oil

½ small yellow onion, finely diced

½ small green bell pepper, finely diced

½ small red bell pepper, finely diced

2 garlic cloves, minced

1 cup long-grain white rice

2 teaspoons kosher salt

1¼ cups vegetable stock or water

½ cup full-fat coconut milk

1 cup frozen peas

Place the oil in a medium saucepan set over medium heat. Once it's hot, add the onion, bell peppers, and garlic. Cook, stirring now and then, until the vegetables are softened, about 10 minutes. Add the rice and salt and cook, stirring now and then, until the rice is opaque and is fragrant, about 1½ minutes. Add the stock and coconut milk and raise the heat to high. Once the mixture comes to a boil, reduce the heat to medium-low and cover the pot. Cook until the rice is tender and all the liquid has been absorbed, about 20 minutes. Stir in the peas, then cover the pot again and turn off the heat. Let the rice sit, covered, for at least 10 minutes before serving. To serve, fluff the rice with a fork and serve warm.

Creamy Spinach and Cheese Grits

These satisfying grits were on our original Key West menu. Serve underneath a pile of grilled shrimp for a fun take on shrimp and grits. To turn these creamy grits into fried grit cakes, pour the cooked grits onto a baking sheet and let them cool. Cut them into squares (or whatever shape you like), dust them with flour, and panfry until crisp on both sides.

2 tablespoons olive oil

1 garlic clove, minced

2 teaspoons Margaritaville House Spice Blend (page 128)

1¼ cups quick-cooking grits

½ cup heavy cream

2 tablespoons unsalted butter

¼ cup cream cheese

½ cup coarsely grated cheddar cheese

One 10-ounce box frozen spinach, thawed, squeezed dry, and coarsely chopped

Place the olive oil in a medium saucepan set over medium heat. Add the garlic and spice blend. Cook, stirring now and then, until the garlic is softened, about 30 seconds.

Add 4 cups water and increase the heat to high. Once the mixture comes to a boil, slowly whisk in the grits and then reduce the heat to low. Simmer the grits, stirring, until they're softened and smooth, about 3 minutes. Add the heavy cream, butter, cream cheese, cheddar cheese, and spinach. Cook, stirring, until the cheddar has melted and the grits are steaming hot, about 3 minutes more. Serve hot.

Skillet Cornbread with Honey Butter

Serves 4

We started making this cornbread at our restaurant in New Orleans. Basically a dessert in disguise, this warm, fluffy, and sweet cornbread was an instant hit with visitors and locals alike. The key is in the hot skillet. It makes the most irresistible crust.

FOR THE HONEY BUTTER

6 tablespoons (¾ stick) unsalted butter, at room temperature

2 tablespoons honey

½ teaspoon kosher salt

FOR THE CORNBREAD

1 cup yellow cornmeal

1 cup all-purpose flour

3 tablespoons sugar

1½ teaspoons baking powder

½ teaspoon baking soda

1 teaspoon kosher salt

8 tablespoons (1 stick) unsalted butter, melted

1½ cups buttermilk

2 large eggs, beaten

MAKE THE HONEY BUTTER: Place the butter, honey, and salt in a small bowl and whisk together. Set aside at room temperature.

MAKE THE CORNBREAD: Preheat the oven to 425°F. Place an 8-inch cast-iron skillet in the oven to heat up.

Place the cornmeal, flour, sugar, baking powder, baking soda, and salt in a medium bowl and whisk together.

Place all but 1 tablespoon of the melted butter in a large bowl and add the buttermilk and eggs. Whisk together until well combined and then gently stir in the cornmeal mixture.

Carefully take the hot skillet out of the oven and add the remaining 1 tablespoon melted butter. Use a brush or a folded paper towel to spread the butter over the surface of the skillet, including the sides. Pour the batter into the hot skillet and return the skillet to the oven. Reduce the oven temperature to 400°F and bake until the cornbread is golden brown, firm to the touch, and a toothpick inserted into the center comes out clean, about 30 minutes.

Serve the cornbread hot, warm, or at room temperature, cut into wedges and slathered with the honey butter.

Grilled Corn with Lime Butter

Serves 4

It's best to make this when corn is in season and is so tender and sweet that it just needs to be kissed by the heat of the grill. If your corn is older and a little starchy, simply blanch it in a pot of boiling water for 2 minutes (or wrap it in damp paper towels and microwave for 2 minutes) before grilling. The lime butter is delicious not only on grilled corn, but also on grilled shrimp or stirred into a pot of cooked rice.

4 tablespoons (½ stick) unsalted butter, at room temperature

Zest of 1 lime

1 tablespoon fresh lime juice

½ teaspoon kosher salt

4 ears corn, husked

2 tablespoons neutral oil (such as canola or vegetable)

Place the butter, lime zest, lime juice, and salt in a small bowl and whisk together. Set aside.

Preheat an outdoor grill to medium or set a grill pan over medium heat. Rub the ears of corn with the oil and grill, turning the ears as they cook, until slightly charred all over. Transfer the corn to a serving platter and slather with the lime butter. Serve hot.

Pickled Jalapeño Mac and Cheese

Not only does this simple cheese sauce make for the easiest ever macaroni and cheese, you can also drizzle it on tortilla chips, baked potatoes, or anywhere else cheese sauce might be welcome (aka everywhere). The pickled jalapeños and their brine cut the richness of the cheese perfectly. Feel free to add more, plus a few dashes of hot sauce if you like things extra spicy, or use less if you prefer things a bit milder.

1½ cups heavy cream

1½ cups coarsely grated white cheddar cheese

1½ cups coarsely grated Monterey Jack cheese

Pinch of cayenne pepper or a few dashes of hot sauce

1 teaspoon garlic powder

Kosher salt

1 tablespoon cornstarch

½ cup drained pickled jalapeños, coarsely chopped, plus 3 tablespoons brine from their jar

1 pound elbow macaroni

Preheat the broiler to high. Position the oven rack so it's 6 inches away from the heating element.

Place the heavy cream, both of the cheeses, the cayenne, garlic powder, and 2 teaspoons salt in a medium saucepan set over high heat. Cook, stirring, until the cheeses melt and the mixture comes to a boil. Immediately reduce the heat to low. Meanwhile, place the cornstarch in a small bowl with 3 tablespoons water and whisk together. Whisk the cornstarch mixture into the simmering sauce and cook until the sauce has thickened, about 1 minute. Stir in the pickled jalapeños and their brine. Keep the sauce warm over low heat.

Meanwhile, bring a large pot of water to a boil and salt it generously. Add the pasta and cook for 2 minutes less than directed on the package to make sure it doesn't end up overcooked. Use a teacup to reserve about 1 cup of the pasta cooking water and drain the pasta in a colander.

Place the cooked pasta back in the pot you cooked it in and add the cheese sauce. Give everything a good stir to combine. If the pasta seems a bit dry, add some of the reserved pasta cooking water to loosen it. Season the pasta with salt and transfer to a baking dish. Broil until the top is bubbling and browned, about 5 minutes. Serve immediately.

Desserts

"NIBBLIN' ON SPONGE CAKE, WATCHIN' THE SUN BAKE . . ."

The only rule in Margaritaville is that there are no rules. Which means if you want to start with dessert, that's fine with us! We keep our dessert menus short and sweet (sorry, couldn't resist) with just a few choices. We love when a table can't decide and ends up with one of everything! Dessert is the easiest way to indulge and relax and we are all for it. This chapter includes our all-time favorite desserts, from classic Key Lime Pie (page 272), which contains a trip to Key West in each slice, to new inventions like our Baked Florida (page 271), our answer to a baked Alaska. There are also desserts geared toward kids (and for adults who are kids at heart) like Crispy Bananarama (page 291) and S'mores Nachos with Warm Chocolate Sauce (page 295). Whether you're a chocoholic or a fruit fanatic (or a little of both), we've got something for you.

Baked Florida

Our answer to a baked Alaska, this dessert has lots of Floridian flavors, including coconut, orange, and pineapple. If you don't have a kitchen torch to brown the meringue, go get one—this is worth it!

1 pint coconut ice cream, slightly softened

1 pint orange sorbet (preferably blood orange), slightly softened

1 cup fresh pineapple cubes, finely chopped

1 small high-quality store-bought pound cake, cut into ½-inch-thick slices

½ cup sugar

3 large egg whites

Pinch of baking soda

1 tablespoon Grand Marnier or triple sec

Line a medium bowl (about 6 inches deep and 8 inches wide on top) with plastic wrap, making sure the plastic covers the entire surface of the bowl and leaves some overhang. Place the coconut ice cream in the bowl and use a rubber spatula to spread it so it's in an even layer. Spread the orange sorbet on top of the coconut ice cream (it's okay if they mix together a bit). Place the pineapple on top of the sorbet in an even layer. Arrange the pound cake slices to form an even layer on top of the pineapple (cut the slices as needed to fit). You might not use all the pound cake, depending on how much you had to start. Wrap the bowl tightly with plastic wrap and place it in the freezer until firm, at least 4 hours or up to 24 hours.

Meanwhile, place the sugar in a small saucepan with 3 tablespoons water. Set the saucepan over high heat and let it come to a boil without stirring. Turn off the heat.

Place the egg whites and baking soda in the bowl of a stand mixer fitted with the whisk attachment (or use a large bowl and a handheld mixer or a whisk and some elbow grease) and beat on high speed until they hold soft peaks, about 3 minutes. Reduce the speed to medium and very slowly drizzle in the sugar syrup. Once all the syrup has been added, raise the speed to high and let the egg whites whirl until they're fluffy and shiny, about 2 minutes. Add the Grand Marnier and whisk just to combine. Transfer the meringue to a pastry bag fitted with a fluted tip (or use a resealable plastic bag and cut off 1 inch from one of the bottom corners).

Remove the bowl from the freezer and unwrap it. Invert the bowl onto a serving platter and peel off the plastic wrap. Pipe the meringue all over the ice cream cake so that the whole thing is beautifully covered with meringue. Pass a kitchen torch over the meringue to toast it and then cut into wedges and serve immediately.

Key Lime Pie

Serves 8 to 10

With us since day one on our original menu, this key lime pie is a keeper. Our crust is a traditional graham cracker crust with the special addition of roasted almonds, which lend flavor and texture, plus a little lime zest to really bring home the lime theme. The filling is pretty straightforward and relies on the inimitable flavor of Nellie & Joe's key lime juice (sold in most grocery stores and also online at keylimejuice.com). If you'd like, feel free to substitute fresh whipped cream for the meringue or just serve the pie unadorned.

Baking spray

¼ cup roasted almonds

1 tablespoon packed dark brown sugar

1½ sleeves graham crackers (7 ounces), crushed into crumbs

½ teaspoon ground cinnamon

1 lime, zest finely grated

6 tablespoons (¾ stick) unsalted butter, melted and cooled

One 14-ounce can sweetened condensed milk

3 large egg yolks

½ cup key lime juice (preferably Nellie & Joe's)

½ cup sugar

3 large egg whites

Pinch of baking soda

1 tablespoon Grand Marnier or triple sec

Preheat the oven to 300°F. Spray a 10-inch pie pan with baking spray.

Place the almonds and brown sugar in a food processor and pulse until finely ground. Add the crushed graham crackers, cinnamon, and lime zest and pulse until everything is finely ground and evenly mixed. Add the melted butter and pulse to combine (the mixture should have the texture of wet sand).

Transfer the graham cracker mixture to the prepared pan and use your fingers or the underside of a measuring cup, along with firm pressure, to press the mixture into an even layer (don't forget about the sides of the pan). Bake the crust until it's a shade darker and it smells wonderful, 20 minutes.

(continued)

Remove the crust from the oven and increase the oven temperature to 350°F. While the oven heats up, let the crust cool.

Place the condensed milk, egg yolks, and key lime juice in a large bowl and whisk together. Pour the filling into the slightly cooled crust. Tap the pie pan on your work surface a couple of times to remove any air bubbles. Bake the pie for 15 minutes and then allow it to cool completely at room temperature.

Once cooled, wrap the pie in plastic wrap and refrigerate until chilled, at least 2 hours and up to 2 days.

Meanwhile, place the sugar in a small saucepan with 3 tablespoons water. Set the saucepan over high heat and let it come to a boil without stirring. Turn off the heat.

Place the egg whites and baking soda in the bowl of a stand mixer fitted with the whisk attachment (or use a large bowl and a handheld mixer or a whisk and some elbow grease) and beat on high speed until they hold soft peaks, about 3 minutes. Reduce the speed to medium and very slowly drizzle in the sugar syrup. Once all the syrup has been added, raise the speed to high and let the egg whites whirl until they're fluffy and shiny, about 2 minutes. Add the Grand Marnier and whisk just to combine.

Spoon the meringue all over the pie in big dollops so that the whole thing is beautifully covered with meringue. If you have one, pass a kitchen torch over the meringue to toast it. Cut into wedges and serve immediately.

Banana Cream Pie with Caramel Rum Sauce

Serves 8 to 10

Our banana cream pie has banana flavor from top to bottom. We blend a whole banana into the graham cracker crust, which lends not only a distinctive flavor, but also helps to bind and sweetened the crushed graham crackers. If you'd like, you could drizzle some melted chocolate on top of this. Yeah, that wouldn't be bad at all. . . .

FOR THE CRUST

Baking spray

1½ sleeves graham crackers (7 ounces), finely crushed into crumbs

1 ripe banana, diced

1 tablespoon packed dark brown sugar

2 tablespoons unsalted butter, melted

FOR THE FILLING

4 large egg yolks

2 cups whole milk

Seeds from 1 vanilla bean, or 2 teaspoons pure vanilla extract

½ cup granulated sugar

¼ cup cornstarch

½ teaspoon kosher salt

2 tablespoons dark rum (optional)

1 cup heavy cream

1 cup sweetened shredded coconut

4 ripe bananas, cut into ½-inch slices

TO SERVE

Caramel Rum Sauce (recipe follows), warmed

MAKE THE CRUST: Preheat the oven to 300°F. Spray a 10-inch pie pan with baking spray.

Place the crushed graham crackers, banana, and brown sugar in a large bowl and use your hands to smash the banana into the crumbs. Knead the mixture until the bananas are broken into pea-size pieces and are evenly distributed. Add the melted butter and mix well to combine (the mixture should have the texture of wet sand). You could also pulse everything together in a food processor if you'd like.

Transfer the graham cracker mixture to the prepared pan and use your fingers or the underside of a measuring cup, along with firm pressure, to press the mixture into an even layer (don't forget about the sides of the pan). Bake the crust until it's a shade darker and it smells wonderful, 20 minutes. Let the crust cool completely while you make the filling.

(continued)

MAKE THE FILLING: Place the egg yolks in a large bowl and whisk them together well.

Place the milk, vanilla, granulated sugar, cornstarch, and salt in a small saucepan set over medium heat. Bring the milk mixture just to a simmer (do not let it boil) and cook, whisking continuously, until bubbles form around the edge. Ladle about 1 cup of the hot milk mixture into the egg yolks and whisk well to combine. Add another ladleful of the hot milk and whisk again (this process will slowly warm the egg yolks instead of blasting them with heat, which would curdle them). Transfer the warmed egg yolk mixture to the pot with the rest of the milk mixture and cook, whisking continuously, until the custard is thick like pudding, about 2 1/2 minutes.

Strain the custard through a fine-mesh sieve (really push it through) into a clean bowl and stir in the rum (if using). Cover the custard with plastic wrap, pressing the plastic directly against the surface of the custard to prevent a skin from forming. Let the custard cool to room temperature and then chill it in the refrigerator for at least 4 hours and up to 24 hours (this cooling process can be sped up by setting the bowl over an even larger bowl of ice water).

Place the cream in the bowl of a stand mixer fitted with a whisk attachment (or use a large bowl and a handheld mixer or a whisk and some elbow grease) and beat until it holds stiff peaks. Carefully fold the whipped cream and the coconut into the cooled custard base.

Place one-third of the cream mixture into the prepared crust and spread to cover. Top evenly with half the banana slices. Carefully spread another third of the cream mixture on top of the bananas and top with the remaining bananas. Spread the remaining cream mixture on top of the bananas. Wrap the pie loosely with plastic wrap and refrigerate until it's quite firm, at least 5 hours and up to 24 hours.

To serve, cut the pie into wedges and serve drizzled with warm Caramel Rum Sauce.

Caramel Rum Sauce

Makes 1 cup

Sort of like a rum butterscotch, this easy dessert sauce is excellent on everything from Banana Cream Pie (page 275) to a simple bowl of vanilla ice cream. If you'd like to make this ahead, simply cool it to room temperature and store it in a jar in the refrigerator for up to a week. To serve, warm it over low heat. This also makes an excellent hostess gift.

½ cup sugar

3 tablespoons spiced or dark rum

½ cup heavy cream

Place the sugar in a heavy-bottomed saucepan and add 2 tablespoons water. Set the saucepan over high heat and cook, swirling the pan but not stirring, until the sugar melts and turns dark amber (like an Irish Setter), about 7 minutes.

Remove the pot from the heat and add the rum and heavy cream (be careful as the caramel will bubble vigorously). Return the pot to the heat and whisk until the sauce is smooth and syrupy, about 1½ minutes.

Keep the sauce warm over low heat.

Coconut Tres Leches Cake

Serves 10 to 12

A combination of traditional tres leches cake and coconut cake, this version is such a keeper. Know when you pour the milks on top of the cake, it will seem like a lot of liquid. Be patient and let everything soak and settle. The result is so wonderful. Once the cake cools to to room temperature, you can cover it with plastic wrap and refrigerate it for up to 2 days before serving.

Baking spray

2 cups all-purpose flour

2 teaspoons baking powder

½ teaspoon kosher salt

8 tablespoons (1 stick) unsalted butter, at room temperature

¾ cup granulated sugar

½ cup whole milk

3 large eggs

1 tablespoon pure vanilla extract

One 13 ½ -ounce can full-fat coconut milk

One 14-ounce can sweetened condensed milk

¼ teaspoon almond extract

1 cup heavy cream

2 tablespoons confectioners' sugar

1 cup sweetened or unsweetened shredded coconut, lightly toasted

Preheat the oven to 350°F. Spray a 9 by 13-inch baking dish with baking spray.

Place the flour, baking powder, and salt in a large bowl and whisk together. Set aside.

Place the butter and granulated sugar in the bowl of a stand mixer fitted with the whisk attachment (or use a large bowl and a handheld mixer or a whisk and some elbow grease). Beat on medium-high speed, stopping to scrape down the sides now and then, until light and airy, about 2 minutes. Add the milk, eggs, and vanilla and beat until thoroughly combined, about 30 seconds.

(continued)

Add the flour mixture to the bowl and use a rubber spatula or a wooden spoon to mix everything together well. Transfer the batter to the prepared baking dish and spread it into an even layer. Bake until golden brown, firm to the touch, and a toothpick inserted into the center comes out clean, about 25 minutes. Place the cake on a wire rack.

Meanwhile, place the coconut milk, sweetened condensed milk, and almond extract in a bowl and whisk together. Use a toothpick or a chopstick to poke about 36 holes all over the surface of the warm cake. Evenly and slowly pour the coconut milk mixture over the surface of the cake. It will seem like a lot of milk, but it will be absorbed! Let the cake cool to room temperature to soak in the milk.

Meanwhile, place the cream and confectioners' sugar in the bowl of a stand mixer fitted with the whisk attachment (or use a large bowl and a handheld mixer or a whisk and some elbow grease) and beat until it holds stiff peaks.

Spread the whipped cream over the surface of the cooled cake and sprinkle with the toasted coconut. Cut into squares (or just use a large spoon to scoop portions) and serve.

Island Rum Cake

Warning: THIS IS AN ADULTS-ONLY CAKE. It's basically a pound cake infused with rum. Lots of rum. Be sure to spray your Bundt pan well with baking spray so the cake will come out easily. Serve this on its own with tea or coffee (or more rum!). While slices are wonderful unadorned, they're really nice topped with whipped cream and fresh raspberries.

Baking spray

2 cups all-purpose flour

¼ cup cornstarch

2 teaspoons baking powder

1 teaspoon kosher salt

8 tablespoons (1 stick) unsalted butter, at room temperature

1 cup granulated sugar

4 large eggs, lightly beaten

¾ cup whole milk

¼ cup vegetable oil

1 tablespoon pure vanilla extract

1¾ cups rum (dark, light, or spiced)

¼ cup packed light brown sugar

Preheat the oven to 325°F. Spray a Bundt pan with baking spray.

Place the flour, cornstarch, baking powder, and salt in a large bowl and whisk together. Set aside.

Place the butter and granulated sugar in the bowl of a stand mixer fitted with the whisk attachment (or use a large bowl and a handheld mixer or a whisk and some elbow grease). Beat on medium-high speed, stopping to scrape down the sides now and then, until light and airy, about 2 minutes. Add the eggs, milk, vegetable oil, vanilla, and 1 cup of the rum and beat until thoroughly combined, about 30 seconds.

Add the dry ingredients to the wet ingredients and use a rubber spatula or a wooden spoon to mix everything together well. Transfer the batter to the prepared Bundt pan. Bake until golden brown, firm to the touch, and a toothpick inserted into the center comes out clean, about 45 minutes. Place the cake on a wire rack.

Meanwhile, place the remaining ¾ cup rum in a small bowl with the brown sugar. Whisk until the sugar has dissolved.

Use a skewer or a chopstick to poke at least 36 holes in the cake. Evenly pour the rum–brown sugar mixture over the surface of the cake. Let the cake cool to room temperature as it absorbs the syrup. The cake is best if you let it sit overnight at room temperature.

Run a butter knife around the edges of the pan to loosen the cake and carefully invert it onto a serving platter. Cut into wedges and serve.

Strawberry Sponge Cake Shortcake

Serves 8 to 10

Part of our anthem, this sponge cake is such a simple and wonderful dessert. You could substitute any berry for the strawberries, or even sliced stone fruit like fresh apricots (as seen in the photo) or plums. A mix is also nice, especially sweet peaches and fresh blueberries.

Baking spray

½ cup all-purpose flour

½ cup cornstarch

4 large eggs, separated

½ teaspoon kosher salt

¾ cup granulated sugar

2 teaspoons pure vanilla extract

3 tablespoons confectioners' sugar, plus extra for serving

1 cup heavy cream

2 cups strawberries, hulled and thinly sliced

Preheat the oven to 350°F. Spray an 8-inch round cake pan with baking spray and line the bottom with a circle of parchment paper cut to fit. Spray the parchment paper just for extra insurance.

Place the flour and cornstarch in a large bowl and whisk together. Set aside.

Place the egg whites, salt, and ¼ cup of the granulated sugar in the bowl of a stand mixer fitted with the whisk attachment (or use a large bowl and a handheld mixer or a whisk and some elbow grease) and beat on high speed until they hold soft peaks, about 1 minute. Transfer the egg white mixture to a separate bowl.

Place the egg yolks, vanilla, and remaining ½ cup granulated sugar in the mixer bowl (no need to clean it first) and beat on high speed until light and fluffy, about 1 minute.

Using a rubber spatula, gently fold the egg white mixture into the egg yolk mixture and then fold in the flour mixture.

Transfer the batter to the prepared cake pan and smooth the surface so the batter is even. Bake the cake until golden brown and a toothpick inserted into the center comes out clean, about 30 minutes. Set the cake on a wire rack and let cool in the pan to room temperature.

(continued)

Meanwhile, place the strawberries in a large bowl and sprinkle with 1 tablespoon of the confectioners' sugar. Toss to combine and let the strawberries sit while the cake cools.

When you're ready to serve the cake, place the cream and the remaining 2 tablespoons confectioners' sugar in the bowl of a stand mixer fitted with the whisk attachment (or use a large bowl and a handheld mixer or a whisk and some elbow grease) and beat until it holds stiff peaks.

Run a butter knife around the edges of the pan to release the cake and then invert it onto a serving platter. Use a serrated knife to cut the cake in half horizontally (as if it were a large sandwich roll). Pick up the top layer of cake and set it aside. Spread the whipped cream on the bottom layer and top with the top half of the cake. Sprinkle the top lightly with confectioners' sugar. Cut into wedges and serve with the strawberries alongside.

Frozen Mango Cheesecake

An easy dessert for a party, this cheesecake can sit in the freezer waiting for you. Serve with extra whipped cream and some fresh sliced mango (or pineapple, kiwi, and/or berries). A few fresh mint leaves are really pretty, too.

FOR THE CRUST

Baking spray

1½ sleeves graham crackers (7 ounces), finely crushed into crumbs

2 tablespoons packed dark brown sugar

5 tablespoons unsalted butter, melted

FOR THE FILLING

One 16-ounce bag frozen mango, defrosted, or 2 ripe mangoes, pitted, peeled, and chopped

Pinch of salt

3 tablespoons key lime juice (preferably Nellie & Joe's) or fresh lime juice

1 cup heavy cream

Two 8-ounce packages cream cheese, at room temperature

1 tablespoon pure vanilla extract

¾ cup confectioners' sugar

MAKE THE CRUST: Preheat the oven to 300°F. Spray a 10-inch pie pan with baking spray.

Place the crushed graham crackers, brown sugar, and butter in a large bowl and mix well to combine (the mixture should have the texture of wet sand).

Transfer the graham cracker mixture to the prepared pan and use your fingers or the underside of a measuring cup, along with firm pressure, to press the mixture into an even layer (don't forget about the sides of the pan). Bake the crust until it's a shade darker and it smells wonderful, 20 minutes. Let the crust cool completely while you make the filling.

MAKE THE FILLING: Place the mango in a blender or food processer with the salt and lime juice and puree until smooth.

(continued)

Place the cream in the bowl of a stand mixer fitted with the whisk attachment (or use a large bowl and a handheld mixer or a whisk and some elbow grease) and beat until it holds stiff peaks. Transfer the whipped cream to another bowl.

Place the cream cheese in the stand mixer bowl (no need to clean it) along with the vanilla and confectioners' sugar. Mix on medium-high speed, stopping to scrape down the sides now and then, until lightened and whipped, about 2 minutes. Add the pureed mango mixture and mix well to combine.

Fold the reserved whipped cream into the cream cheese mixture in thirds (this way, you won't lose all the air you worked hard to create in the whipped cream).

Pour the filling into the prepared crust and spread it into an even layer. Place the cheesecake in the freezer. Freeze until firm, at least 4 hours (or you can make it up to 3 days ahead, but be sure to cover it tightly with plastic wrap after it's frozen solid).

To serve, take the cheesecake out of the freezer and let it sit for 15 minutes to defrost slightly. Cut into wedges and serve.

Crispy Bananarama

Although unexpected, this dessert is the biggest hit ever with kids (and adults, too!). Flour tortillas get covered with chocolate spread and wrapped around bananas. Quickly fried until crisp, these turn into chocolate-banana almost-taquitos that are best served hot with a scoop of vanilla ice cream. Yum!

¼ cup chocolate hazelnut spread (preferably Nutella)

Two 10-inch flour tortillas

2 ripe bananas

1 teaspoon ground cinnamon

Neutral oil (such as canola or vegetable), for frying

2 tablespoons hazelnuts, coarsely chopped

1 tablespoon finely grated zest orange zest

Spread half of the chocolate spread evenly on each tortilla. Place one banana on each tortilla and sprinkle each banana with ½ teaspoon of the cinnamon. Roll each tortilla tightly, tucking in the edges as if you were making banana burritos. Secure each tortilla with a couple of toothpicks.

Pour 1 inch of oil into a large heavy pot and heat the oil over medium heat. Test the oil: When one of the tortillas sizzles upon contact, it's ready. Place both of the rolled tortillas into the oil, seam-side down. Cook, turning the rolled tortillas a few times while they cook, until golden brown all over, about 4 minutes. Transfer the rolled tortillas to a paper towel–lined plate to drain. Remove and discard the toothpicks and cut each tortilla crosswise into bite-sized pieces. Sprinkle the hazelnuts and orange zest over the pieces. Serve immediately.

Chocolate-Bourbon Croissant Bread Pudding

Serves 8 to 10

A version of this bread pudding was on our original menu. Carlo helped us elevate it by using really high-quality dark chocolate and bourbon and swapping out regular bread for golden croissants. Toasting the croissants before mixing them with the custard not only deepens their flavor, but also dries them out, which makes them able to soak up the delicious custard.

1 pound croissants, torn into bite-size pieces

2 cups heavy cream

2 cups whole milk

¼ cup sweetened condensed milk

1 tablespoon pure vanilla extract

¼ cup packed dark brown sugar

¼ cup granulated sugar

3 large eggs

2 tablespoons bourbon

1 tablespoon unsalted butter

½ cup finely chopped high-quality dark chocolate or dark chocolate chips, plus extra for serving

Vanilla ice cream, for serving

Preheat the oven to 300°F.

Place the croissant pieces on a baking sheet and bake, stirring them now and then, until golden brown and crisp, about 20 minutes. Set the croissants aside to cool. Leave the oven on.

Place the heavy cream, milk, sweetened condensed milk, vanilla, and sugars in a medium pot set over medium heat. Stir the mixture as it heats to dissolve the sugars. Once bubbles form around the edge of the pan, turn off the heat.

Place the eggs in a large bowl and whisk well to combine. While whisking, ladle in about 1 cup of the hot cream mixture and then repeat until you've added all the hot cream mixture (this keeps the eggs from scrambling). Whisk in the bourbon. Add the toasted croissant pieces to the bowl and stir well to combine. Let the mixture sit for about 10 minutes to let the croissants absorb the custard.

Use the butter to grease a 9 by 13-inch baking dish. Add half the croissant mixture to the dish and then sprinkle with half the chocolate. Repeat once more.

Bake the bread pudding until it's golden brown, slightly puffed up, and set throughout (test by jiggling the baking dish), about 40 minutes. Cut into squares and serve warm topped with vanilla ice cream and chopped chocolate.

S'mores Nachos with Warm Chocolate Sauce

Serves 8 to 10

When you don't have access to a real campfire to make s'mores, try these "nachos." You just lay graham crackers on a baking sheet, top them with marshmallows, and run the whole thing under the broiler to bronze the marshmallows (or burn them, whatever is your pleasure). Drizzled with a warm chocolate sauce, these are irresistible. Feel free to add more toppings, like Caramel Rum Sauce (page 278), chopped nuts, chopped dark chocolate, toasted coconut flakes, sliced bananas, crushed pretzels, or even a generous sprinkle of flaky sea salt.

½ cup heavy cream

½ tablespoon unsalted butter

½ cup semisweet chocolate chips

Two 4½-ounce sleeves graham crackers, broken into halves

One 10-ounce bag mini marshmallows

Preheat the broiler to low. Position the oven rack so it's 6 inches away from the heating element.

Bring a small saucepan of water to a boil and then reduce the heat to maintain a simmer. Place the cream, butter, and chocolate chips in a large heatproof bowl and set it over the saucepan (make sure the bottom of the bowl doesn't touch the water). Stir the mixture until the butter and chocolate have melted, about 5 minutes. Turn off the heat but leave the bowl over the saucepan to keep the sauce warm.

Place half the graham cracker halves on a baking sheet and top with half the marshmallows. Broil just until the marshmallows turn golden brown, about 1 minute, depending on the strength of your broiler. Place the remaining graham crackers and marshmallows on top and broil one more time until the second layer of marshmallows is golden brown (or burnt, if you prefer that!), about 1 minute more.

Drizzle the warm chocolate sauce over the nachos and serve straight from the pan, with plenty of napkins handy.

Drinks

"IT'S ONLY HALF PAST TWELVE, BUT I DON'T CARE—IT'S FIVE O'CLOCK SOMEWHERE...."

If you have a bar in your house or a Frozen Concoction Maker on your counter, you are already speaking our language. In Margaritaville, the drinks are plentiful and always perfectly tuned into the moment. From morning drinks like the Perfect Bloody Marias (page 302) and Brunch Rum Punch (page 301) to over half a dozen types of margaritas and specialty cocktails, there's something for all hours of the day in this chapter. There are also beer drinks (micheladas!), wine drinks (sangria!), and even a variety of nonalcoholic drinks (pink lemonade!) so there's truly something for everyone and every taste. Many of these drinks can be turned into frozen concoctions if you have one of our Frozen Concoction Makers. Simply fill the ice reservoir with ice and place all the liquid ingredients into the glass jar. Concoct until smooth and then serve. This works well with Brunch Rum Punch (page 301), Pineapple Rum Runners (page 301), all the margaritas, as well as the 5 o'Clock Somewhere (page 313) and the Incommunicado (page 305).

Brunch Rum Punch

With a perfectly balanced mix of light and dark rums and all our favorite juices, this punch makes every brunch very special. If you want to make it a little less strong (that way, you can enjoy more!), just add 2 cups sparkling water. The Pineapple Run Runners variation is named for rum-running, another term for bootlegging, especially if brought over water. While we never condone breaking the law, we always like the idea of bringing a drink anywhere near the water.

½ cup light rum (preferably Margaritaville Silver Rum)

½ cup dark rum (preferably Margaritaville Dark Rum)

¾ cup fresh orange juice

¾ cup pineapple juice

¾ cup cranberry juice

2 tablespoons grenadine

Ice

4 orange slices

Place the rums, orange juice, pineapple juice, cranberry juice, and grenadine in a large pitcher and stir together. Fill four tall glasses with ice and divide the rum mixture among them. Garnish each glass with an orange slice and serve immediately.

Pineapple Rum Runners: Mix together 2 cups pineapple juice and ¼ cup grenadine with ½ cup light rum (preferably Margaritaville Silver Rum), ½ cup dark rum (preferably Margaritaville Dark Rum), and ½ cup fresh lime juice. Serve in glasses filled with crushed ice and garnish with fresh pineapple wedges.

Perfect Bloody Marias

Bloody Marias are the classic brunch drink remixed (literally) with lots of fresh lime juice and tequila instead of the more traditional vodka. These are the best accompaniment to South Florida Eggs Benedict (page 23) or your favorite decadent breakfast.

4 cups tomato juice

2 tablespoons prepared horseradish

1 tablespoon Worcestershire sauce

¼ cup fresh lime juice

1 cup silver tequila (preferably Margaritaville Silver Tequila)

1 teaspoon kosher salt

Ice

4 celery stalks

4 lime slices

Place the tomato juice, horseradish, Worcestershire, lime juice, tequila, and salt in a large pitcher and stir together. Fill four tall glasses with ice and divide the tomato mixture among them. Garnish each glass with a celery stalk and a lime slice and serve immediately.

Cajun Bloody Marys: Swap in lemon juice for the lime juice, vodka for the tequila, and 2 tablespoons Cajun seasoning for the salt. Add a splash of brine from a jar of pickled okra and garnish with pickled okra instead of celery and lemon wedges instead of lime wedges.

LandShark Micheladas

Serves 4

LandShark is so light and refreshing, which makes it a great everyday beer but also means it combines well with other flavors. Micheladas, which are basically half tomato juice and half beer seasoned with some lime and chile, are just the thing to showcase how versatile Land-Shark is. Serve with Huevos Rancheros (page 16).

4 cups tomato juice

1 tablespoon Worcestershire sauce

1 tablespoon hot sauce (preferably Tabasco)

½ cup key lime juice (preferably Nellie & Joe's) or fresh lime juice

Ice

4 LandShark Lagers

Place the tomato juice, Worcestershire, hot sauce, and key lime juice in a large pitcher and stir together.

Fill four tall glasses with ice and divide the tomato juice mixture among them. Top each one with some beer and stir together with a spoon. Serve immediately with whatever beer is left in the bottles so you and your friends can top off your drinks as you sip.

Incommunicado

We raided the liquor cabinet for this drink. More than one will leave you . . . incommunicado.

Ice, preferably crushed

1 tablespoon aged tequila (preferably Margaritaville Gold Tequila)

1 tablespoon light rum (preferably Margaritaville Silver Rum)

1 tablespoon triple sec (preferably Margaritaville Triple Sec)

1 tablespoon vodka

1 teaspoon grenadine

2 tablespoons pineapple juice

2 tablespoons cranberry juice

2 tablespoons fresh lime juice

Fill a tall shaker with ice and pour in all the ingredients. Shake well to combine and then pour everything, ice and all, into a tall glass. Serve immediately.

Jimmy's Perfect Margarita

Serves 1, easily multiplied

"Some people claim that there's a woman to blame, but I know it's my own damn fault. . . ."

While there's no fault in this margarita, there's a lot to love. It's our definitive house margarita and is the perfect balance of tart lime juice, sweet triple sec, and biting tequila.

Kosher salt

1 lime wedge

Ice, preferably crushed

¼ cup aged tequila (preferably Margaritaville Gold Tequila)

2 tablespoons triple sec (preferably Margaritaville Triple Sec)

1 tablespoon superfine sugar

3 tablespoons fresh lime juice

Place a layer of salt on a small plate. Rub the lime wedge around the rim of a tall glass and then tip the glass upside down onto the plate of salt and coat the rim with salt. Reserve the lime wedge.

Fill a cocktail shaker with ice and add the tequila, triple sec, sugar, lime juice, and 3 tablespoons water. Shake vigorously to combine and then pour the mixture, ice and all, into the prepared glass. Garnish with the reserved lime wedge and serve immediately.

Ginger Citrus Margaritas: Shake together ¼ cup fresh lime juice, ¼ cup agave nectar, and ¼ cup orange juice with 1 cup aged tequila (preferably Margaritaville Gold Tequila) and 2 cups spicy ginger beer. Stir together and serve in glasses filled with crushed ice (salt the rims first, if you'd like!). Garnish with slices of fresh lime and orange and candied ginger, too.

"Feelin' Hot Hot Hot" Jalapeño Margaritas: Place 1 thinly sliced jalapeño in a small bowl with 1 cup silver tequila (preferably Margaritaville Silver Tequila). Cover and refrigerate for at least 6 hours and up to 24 hours. Strain the tequila into a pitcher and reserve the jalapeño slices. Shake the tequila together with ¼ cup agave nectar, ½ cup fresh lime juice, and ½ cup triple sec (preferably Margaritaville Triple Sec). Serve in glasses filled with crushed ice (salt the rims first, if you'd like!). Garnish with lime wedges and the reserved jalapeño slices.

Frozen Paradise Palomas

Serves 4

Typically made with grapefruit soda, we love making palomas with freshly squeezed grapefruit and lime juices, and a little agave nectar for sweetness. We throw everything in a blender or a Frozen Concoction Maker to make the most deliciously tart frozen drink ever. You could substitute freshly squeezed blood orange juice or tangerine juice for a fun alternative.

¼ cup fresh lime juice

¼ cup agave nectar

1 cup silver tequila (preferably Margaritaville Silver Tequila)

2 cups fresh ruby red grapefruit juice (or high quality store-bought)

3 cups ice cubes

4 grapefruit slices

Place the lime juice, agave nectar, tequila, grapefruit juice, and ice in a blender (or place the liquids in the container of a Frozen Concoction Maker and fill the hopper with ice) and puree until smooth. Divide the mixture among four glasses and garnish each drink with a slice of grapefruit. Serve immediately.

Very Berry Frozen Margaritas: Substitute 1 cup fresh orange juice and 1½ cups fresh berries for the grapefruit juice.

Key West Coconut and Lime Frozen Margaritas: Blend together ½ cup aged tequila (preferably Margaritaville Gold Tequila), ½ cup coconut rum (preferably Margaritaville Coconut Rum), 1 cup light coconut milk, ½ cup unsweetened coconut flakes, ¼ cup key lime juice (preferably Nellie & Joe's), ¼ cup fresh orange juice, 4 dashes of grenadine, and 3 cups ice cubes (or place the liquids in the container of a Frozen Concoction Maker and fill the hopper with ice). Divide the mixture among four glasses and serve immediately.

Frozen Watermelon and Mint Margaritas: Blend together 3 cups bite-size cubes watermelon, a small handful of fresh mint leaves, ½ cup fresh lime juice, ¼ cup agave nectar, 1 cup silver tequila (preferably Margaritaville Silver Tequila), and 3 cups ice cubes (or place the liquids in the container of a Frozen Concoction Maker and fill the hopper with ice). Divide the mixture among four glasses and serve immediately. Garnish each with a wedge of watermelon and a fresh mint sprig.

5 o'Clock Somewhere

Similar to a Long Island Iced Tea, this mixture of citrus juices, tequila, and rum is definitely "somethin' tall an' strong. . . ." We love this drink, and the song its name comes from so much, that we named one of our bars after it.

¼ cup light rum (preferably Margaritaville Silver Rum)

1 tablespoon passion fruit tequila
(preferably Margaritaville Passion Fruit Tequila) or silver tequila

2 tablespoons fresh orange juice

2 tablespoons pineapple juice

1 tablespoon fresh lemon juice

1 tablespoon grenadine

Ice, preferably crushed

1 orange wedge

1 cocktail cherry

Place the rum, tequila, orange juice, pineapple juice, lemon juice, and grenadine in a shaker with some ice and shake well to combine. Fill a tall glass with ice and strain the mixture into it. Garnish with the orange wedge and the cherry. Serve immediately.

Red Wine and Cherry Sangria

Serves 4 to 6

Our version of classic sangria involves no sickeningly sweet mix-ins or anything like that. We fill ours with fresh fruit and make it light with a little sparking water. Make sure you use a wine you would enjoy drinking on its own in order to have the best-quality sangria.

One 750-ml bottle fruity, full-bodied red wine

¼ cup triple sec (preferably Margaritaville Triple Sec)

1 cup sparkling water

1 navel orange, ends discarded, thinly sliced

1 lemon, ends discarded, thinly sliced

2 cups fresh cherries, pitted and halved, or one 10-ounce bag frozen cherries, defrosted and halved

1 large cinnamon stick

Ice (optional)

Place the wine, triple sec, sparkling water, orange and lemon slices, cherries, and cinnamon stick in a large bowl or pitcher and stir well to combine. Refrigerate until chilled and the flavors are well combined, at least 3 hours and up to 24 hours. Remove and discard the cinnamon stick. Serve chilled in glasses with ice, if you'd like. Be sure to distribute the fruit among the glasses.

White Wine and Peach Sangria: **Substitute a bottle of full-bodied white wine for the red wine and 2 ripe peaches cut into wedges for the cherries. Leave everything else the same.**

Cucumber and Mint Coolers

Serves 4

Completely stunning, these drinks are also amazingly thirst-quenching. The strips of cucumber not only look beautiful, they're also a refreshing snack. If you'd prefer to make this alcoholic, try adding gin for a twist on a gin and tonic.

2 large cucumbers

½ cup fresh mint leaves

½ cup fresh lime juice

3 tablespoons agave nectar

4 cups sparkling water

Ice, preferably crushed

Coarsely chop one of the cucumbers and place it in a blender with the mint, lime juice, and agave nectar. Blend until smooth. Pass the mixture through a fine-mesh sieve into a large pitcher. Add the sparkling water and stir to combine.

Use a vegetable peeler to slice the second cucumber into long strips. Place a few strips into each of four tall glasses and then fill each glass with ice. Divide the drink among the glasses. Serve immediately.

Watermelon Pink Lemonade

Serves 4

Adored by kids and adults alike, this summery drink gets its hue from plenty of fresh watermelon and a splash of grenadine for good measure. If you'd like this completely smooth, strain the watermelon mixture through a fine-mesh sieve.

3 cups bite-size cubes watermelon

½ cup fresh lemon juice

½ cup agave nectar

2 tablespoons grenadine

Ice, preferably crushed

Place the watermelon, lemon juice, agave nectar, and grenadine into a blender and puree until smooth. Transfer to a pitcher and stir in 2 cups water.

Fill four tall glasses with ice and divide the lemonade among them. Serve immediately.

Tailgating

Twenty Party and Menu Suggestions

BACKYARD BEACH BARBECUE

When you can't get to the beach, create your own in the backyard. Set up Adirondack chairs in a large sandbox so that you can eat with your toes in the sand. No shirt, no shoes, no problem. Flip-flops are welcome. Eat under a beach umbrella and lay out beach towels for the kids.

Grilled Oysters with Tarragon Butter (page 40)
JWB Lobster Rolls (page 155)
Baby Back Ribs with Guava Barbecue Sauce
   (page 228)
Cilantro-Lime Coleslaw (page 242)
Grilled Corn with Lime Butter (page 263)
Strawberry Sponge Cake Shortcake (page 285)
Frozen Watermelon and Mint Margaritas (page 311)
Watermelon Pink Lemonade (page 317)

COASTAL MEXICAN DINNER

When a trip to Mexico isn't coming up in your calendar, transport yourself there through your kitchen. Get a traditional molcajete for your guacamole and turn up the mariachi music. Order papel picado flags online and string them in your dining room or outside over the deck.

Guacamole (page 241) with tortilla chips
Veracruz Seafood Cocktail (page 68)
Seared Grouper with Fresh Mango Salsa (page 206)
Frozen Paradise Palomas (page 311)
Cucumber and Mint Coolers (page 317)

BIG GAME PARTY

No matter which team you're cheering for, you're going to need something good to eat and plenty to drink. Decorate with team colors, buy inexpensive trophy cups to hold chips and snacks, get huge foam fingers for all your guests, and do the wave!

Volcano Nachos (page 36)
Pimiento Cheese Hushpuppies (page 77)
Spicy Buffalo Chicken Wings with Buttermilk Blue
   Cheese Dressing (page 94)
Sweet Chile Chicken Wings (page 97)
Beach Club Sandwich (page 146), cut into quarters
Frozen Paradise Palomas (page 311)
Cold LandShark Lagers
Iced tea

A DAY ON THE BOAT

The best meals are the ones enjoyed when you're surrounded with water. Whether you have an actual boat or just want to pretend you're on one, pack your coolers and don't forget your sunscreen.

Cuban Meat Loaf Survival Sandwiches (page 140)
Tostones with Mojo Sauce (page 84)
Guacamole (page 241) with tortilla chips
Frozen Paradise Palomas (page 311)
Cucumber and Mint Coolers (page 317)

PARAKEET BIRTHDAY PARTY

There's nothing like food for a kids' party that everyone can enjoy. This menu will make everyone happy! Make sure to include games and activities like a piñata, a scavenger hunt, or a potato sack race. Or, better yet, do a craft project that can occupy the kids and double as a party favor (like macaroni necklaces or tie-dyed T-shirts).

Cajun Chicken Quesadilla (page 91), cut into
   small wedges
Aloha Hot Dogs (page 156)
Own-Damn-Fault Hot Dogs (page 158)
Blackened Chili Dogs (page 159)
S'mores Nachos with Warm Chocolate Sauce (page
   295)
Key West Coconut and Lime Frozen Margaritas
   (page 311), for the parents
Watermelon Pink Lemonade (page 317)

PARAKEET PIZZA PARTY

If you have a kid who loves to be in the kitchen, there's nothing better than making pizza together! Gather some of their friends, make the easiest dough (thanks, Carlo!), and set out toppings so they can all mix and match and customize their own pizzas. Order kids' chef hats online to make them feel extra professional!

JWB Caesar Salad with Sourdough Croutons
   (page 102)
Pizza à la Minute (page 230)
Various pizza toppings (tomato sauce, cheese,
   sausage, etc.)
Red wine, for the adults
Watermelon Pink Lemonade (page 317)

MARGARITA HAPPY HOUR

Whatever time your friends are coming over, remember that it's always at five o'clock somewhere. Fire up your Frozen Concoction Maker and always remember: there's no such thing as too much ice. This menu is all handheld and easy to eat around a huge coffee table, indoors or outside.

Pimiento Cheese Hushpuppies (page 77)
Peel-and-Eat Shrimp (page 41)
Conch Fritters with Calypso Sauce (page 48)
Ginger Citrus Margaritas (page 306)
Jimmy's Perfect Margarita (page 306)
Cucumber and Mint Coolers (page 317)

NOLA BIG EASY PARTY

Dreaming about the last Mardi Gras you went to? Relive the fun in your own home! Decorate with Mardi Gras beads. Set the buffet table with overlapping purple, green, and yellow tablecloths and get napkins in the same colors. Put a sign on your front door that reads Bourbon Street and turn up the jazz!

Tailgate Muffuletta for a Crowd (page 145)
Outside-Optional Cajun Clambake (page 199)
Chocolate-Bourbon Croissant Bread Pudding
   (page 292)
Cajun Bloody Marys (page 302)
Sweet iced tea

DOCKSIDE DINNER

Whether you live near a lake, river, bay, or beach, as long as you have a good seafood shop in your area, you can always dine dockside. Extend the nautical theme to your table with cleaned oyster shells to hold salt and pepper and rope to tie your napkins.

Kusshi Oysters with Granny Smith, Cucumber, and
   Mint Granita (page 67)
Outside-Optional Cajun Clambake (page 199)
A big green salad
Frozen Mango Cheesecake (page 287)
Cold white wine
Sparkling water with lemon

KINDA HEALTHY BRUNCH

Whether you enjoy this menu on a weekend morning after a long run on the beach or after a big night on the town, there's a lot to feel virtuous about. Decorate the table with big bowls of citrus and put a few slices of cucumber in your water pitcher for an extra spa-like effect.

Pineapple and Coconut Milk Smoothie (page 287)
Huevos Rancheros (page 16)
Avocado and Papaya Salad with Spicy Lime Dressing
   (page 108)
LandShark Micheladas (page 304)
Freshly squeezed grapefruit juice

DECADENT BRUNCH

When you've got time to linger at brunch all afternoon, this is the menu to make. Make sure to squeeze the orange juice and turn on the coffee just before your guests arrive so the aromas fill the air.

South Florida Eggs Benedict (page 23)
Best-Ever French Toast (page 28)
Perfect Bloody Marias (page 302)
Brunch Rum Punch (page 301)
Freshly squeezed orange juice and hot coffee

DOWN HOME PARTY

This is for when you want some country-style cooking even if you're in a city or on the beach. Put on some country music, buy a case of mason jars to use as glasses, and use bandanas for napkins.

Pimiento Cheese Hushpuppies (page 77)
Jalapeño Deviled Eggs with Pickled Mustard Seeds
   (page 88)
Buttermilk Fried Chicken with Country Gravy
   (page 192)
Skillet Cornbread with Honey Butter (page 260)
Sautéed greens
Banana Cream Pie with Caramel Rum Sauce
   (page 275)
Cold LandShark Lagers
Watermelon Pink Lemonade (page 317)

LUXE-CASUAL TACO FIESTA

When you've got friends coming over for a relaxed taco party but you want to really impress them, try this menu. You can put out all of the toppings plus the shrimp and pork and everyone can build their own.

Fried Green Tomato Salad with Salsa Verde and
   Queso Fresco (page 112)
Belizean Shrimp Ceviche (page 76)
Slow Cooker Pork Shoulder with LandShark and
   Cola (page 180)
Warm tortillas, diced onions, chopped cilantro, and
   lime wedges
Coconut Tres Leches Cake (page 279)
LandShark Micheladas (page 304)
"Feelin' Hot Hot Hot" Jalapeño Margaritas
   (page 306)
Iced hibiscus tea with lime

STEAKHOUSE-AT-HOME DINNER

When you want all the festivity and flair of a steakhouse without actually having to leave your home, this menu will deliver. Don't forget to starch that white tablecloth!

Little Gem Wedge Salad (page 107)
Prime Sirloin Oscar (page 172)
Lobster Hash Browns with Jalapeño Cheese
   (page 250)
JWB Creamed Spinach (page 253)
Baked Florida (page 271)
Rich red wine
Cucumber and Mint Coolers (page 317)

EASY WEEKNIGHT DINNER

We believe that you can be in Margaritaville anytime, including on a busy weekday. Let this easy-to-prepare menu transport you somewhere relaxed even on a school night.

Seared Grouper with Fresh Mango Salsa
   (page 206)
Cooked rice and roasted asparagus
White Wine and Peach Sangria (page 314)
Sparkling water

ANOTHER EASY WEEKNIGHT DINNER

As Jimmy says, "There are good days and bad days and going-half-mad days." Serve this simple meal for your family when you want something comforting and as easy to eat as it is to make.

Margaritaville Family Recipe Cuban Meat Loaf
   (page 167)
Island Rice Pilaf (page 256)
A big green salad
Cold LandShark Lagers
Iced tea

ITALIAN WINE PARTY

When you have lots of bottles of Italian wine to drink, invite all your friends over to try them and put out a spread of snacks that can double as a light meal. Set the table with a red-checkered tablecloth and use Italian tomato cans (emptied and rinsed) as vases for flowers.

JWB Caesar Salad dressing (page 102) with romaine
    leaves for dipping
Hollywood Burrata with Grated Tomato Dressing
    (page 87) with crostini
Crispy Calamari with Peppadews and Lemon Aioli
    (page 57)
Fried Baby Artichokes with Remoulade (page 83)
Lots of Italian red wine and prosecco
Sparkling water

PAELLA PARTY

Make this menu, and you'll find your home has turned into a Spanish seaside town. Round out the meal with lots of Spanish cheeses, cured ham, and olives and get all your guests small tins of pimentón, Spanish smoked sweet paprika, to take home as gifts.

Andalusian Gazpacho (page 115)
Spanish Octopus Salad (page 51)
Paella del Mar (page 222)
Red Wine and Cherry Sangria (page 314)
White Wine and Peach Sangria (page 314)
Lemonade

COME BACK TO JAMAICA

"We had only come for chicken," Jimmy explains in "Jamaica Mistaica." And here it is! For an instant trip to the Caribbean, enjoy this meal outside with lots of friends. Play some reggae, serve the drinks in pineapples, and kick back while the chicken finishes on the grill.

Jerk Chicken (page 190)
Island Rice Pilaf (page 256)
Cilantro-Lime Coleslaw (page 242)
Plantain Chips (page 72)
Island Rum Cake (page 282)
Jamaican beer
Pineapple Rum Runners (page 301)
Iced hibiscus tea

BUILD-YOUR-OWN BURGER PARADISE

For a really fun party with lots of friends who all like something different, grill a bunch of beef, turkey, and veggie burgers and set out all the toppings you can think of so that everyone can build their own burgers. With a big batch of Oven Fries and lots of cold LandShark Lager, you'll surely be in paradise.

Cheeseburgers in Paradise with Paradise Island
    Dressing (page 129)
Black-and-Blue Burgers (page 131)
Turkey Burgers with Cheddar and Barbecue Aioli
    (page 132)
JWB Surf 'n' Turf Burgers (page 135)
Ultimate Veggie Burgers (page 136)
Oven Fries (page 254)
Cold LandShark Lagers
Watermelon Pink Lemonade (page 317)

Recipes Organized by Fun!

FOOD TO BRING TO OR MAKE ON THE BEACH!

DRINKS TO THROW IN THE FROZEN CONCOCTION MAKER!

ELEVATED FOOD FROM AND INSPIRED BY JWB!

FOOD FOR FAMILIES AND LARGE GROUPS!

KINDA HEALTHY FOOD!

"I treat my body like a temple, you treat yours
like a tent"

Ten Practical Party Tips

1   **HAVE FUN WITH INVITATIONS!** They help get the party started before it even begins. A text or an e-mail will get the word out, but how much more fun does a treasure map with the party details written on it sound?

2   **MAKE DESSERT FIRST!** A cake on the counter or a freezer stocked with ice cream means you can cross something substantial off of your to-do list—plus, you're guaranteed something delicious no matter what.

3   **DON'T FORGET ABOUT THE MUSIC!** It sets the tone for the whole party. May we suggest a certain station called Radio Margaritaville . . . ?

4   **FOR A PORTABLE PARTY, MIX LARGE BATCHES OF DRINKS IN GALLON WATER JUGS!** That way, you don't have to bring multiple bottles of things or anything to measure. Just pick up a bag of ice on your way to your friend's house, a tailgate party, the beach, or wherever the party is.

5   **SPEAKING OF ICE, YOU CAN NEVER HAVE TOO MUCH!** Always buy an extra bag or ask a friend to bring some.

6   **DIVIDE AND CONQUER THE FOOD!** Assign side dishes, drinks, and dessert. Or have a competition (best macaroni and cheese!) and have everyone bring his or her own version. It's not only fun, it also means you don't have to do all the cooking.

7   **BE CREATIVE WITH DECORATIONS!** If you're having everyone over to watch a game, get paper napkins with the team colors and banners with the names. Or if you're having a pool party, fill the pool with colorful floats.

8   **PLAN AHEAD!** Empty your dishwasher before the party so you have a place for dirty dishes. Or if you're partying at the beach, bring trash bags so you leave only your footprints.

9   **LIGHTS, CAMERA, ACTION!** Lighting makes a big difference in setting the tone, and it doesn't need to be complicated. If you're outside, string some lights outside and fire up a few lanterns. If you're inside, turn off big bright overhead lights and use lamps and candles.

10   **THINK OF TOMORROW. . . !** Stock up on containers so you can send friends home with leftovers.

Acknowledgments

Special thanks to: Dan Leonard, Brad Schwaeble, and Mark Rogers, for always understanding the importance of this book and allowing me to dedicate the time needed to the project. The Margaritaville Hollywood Beach Culinary Team, for the support during the "excruciating" photo shoot! John Dickenson, for the hard work of keeping our unique lionfish spearfishing program alive. Louisa Cohlan, for coming up with the original idea for this cookbook and for recommending me as the face of the cookbook. John and Jimmy, for trusting me with this amazing and ambitious project.

And one more extra special thanks to Tamara Baldanza-Dekker (Tamarita) and Courtney Griffith: not only did you have the patience to deal with me but you made the book and all its moving parts happen. You are the authors of this book, and I am an accessory!

—CARLO SERNAGLIA

Thanks to everyone at Margaritaville, and to Kari Stuart and Esther Newberg, and to my wife, Grace.

—JULIA TURSHEN

Thanks to Bella and Bobby Patterson; Knox Hinson; R.J. Maya; Nico, Cristina, and Leonie Meyart and all of their parents. And a big fins up to the Margaritaville Hollywood Hotel Beach Resort and its staff! Also, thanks to our capable literary agents, Esther Newberg and Kari Stuart of International Creative Management.

—MARGARITAVILLE

Index